BURGOS
CATHEDRAL

Editor in chief: Vicente Pastor

Layout: V. Pastor and J. Alegre
Photomechanics: Base5
Photocomposition: LetterMAC
Printed by: G. Otzarreta

Translated from Spanish by: Gordon Keitch

Photographs: Norberto
      Imagen M.A.S. (Págs. 3, 4, 8, 10, 13, 17, 30c, 35, 36b, 42a, 47, 56-57, 60, 63, 66c, 87, 91a, 94a, 97)

This book was written in collaboration with the Dean and Chapter of Burgos Cathedral

© *Text:* Salvador Andrés Ordax

© EDILESA
  General Sanjurjo, 7 - 24001-León, Spain
  Teléfono: (987) 22 10 66

  I.S.B.N.: 84-8012-043-6
  Depósito Legal: SS-434/93
  Printed in Spain. Impreso en España

BURGOS
CATHEDRAL

World Heritage

Text by
SALVADOR ANDRES ORDAX

Photographs by
NORBERTO
IMAGEN M.A.S.

Edilesa

CONTENTS

BURGOS AND ITS CATHEDRAL 7

THE BUILDING 13

THE OUTSIDE OF THE CATHEDRAL 19

The West Face: The Royal Door 19

The South Face: The *Sarmental* Door 23

The North Face: The *Coronería* Door 29

The Apse of the Cathedral: The *Pellejería* Door 33

ART INSIDE 34

The Nave 36

The Northern Aisle of the Nave 49

The Northern Arm of the Transept 55

The Northern Side of the Ambulatory 58

Reliefs and Sculptures in the Retrochoir and Ambulatory 63

The Chapel of the Purification or High Constable's Chapel 66

The Southern Side of the Ambulatory 76

The Southern Arm of the Transept 81

The Southern Aisle of the Nave 86

Cloister and Museum 92

BIBLIOGRAPHY 103

GROUNDPLAN OF BURGOS CATHEDRAL

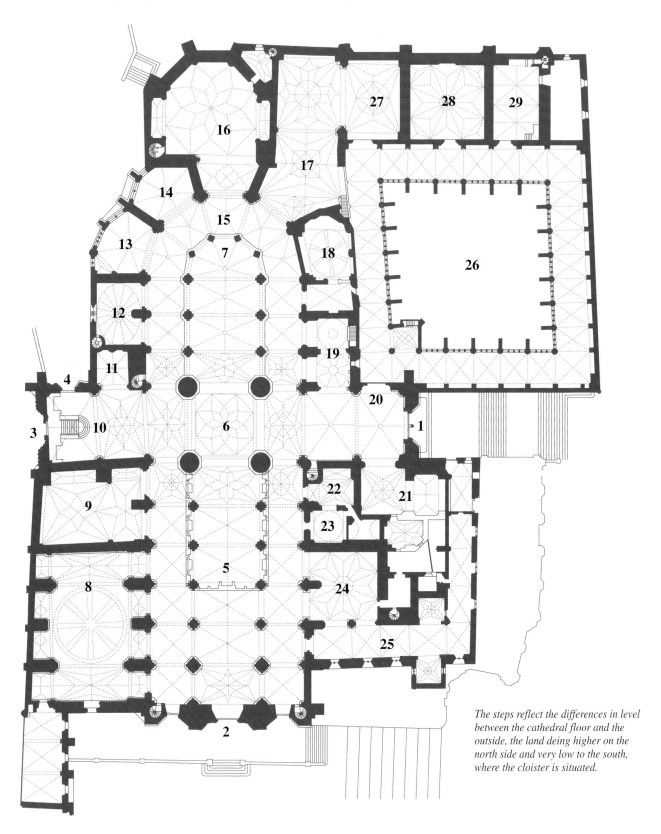

The steps reflect the differences in level between the cathedral floor and the outside, the land deing higher on the north side and very low to the south, where the cloister is situated.

1. *Sarmental* Door
2. The Royal Door of Pardon, or St Mary's Door
3. The Apostles' Door, or *Puerta de la Coronería*
4. Skinners' Door *(Puerta de la Pellejería)*
5. Chapter Choir
6. Transept and Tambour
7. Chancel
8. St Tecla's Chapel
9. Chapel of the Conception, or St. Anne's Chapel
10. Golden Stairway

11. St. Nicholas's Chapel
12. Chapel of the Nativity
13. Chapel of the Annunciation
14. St. Gregory's Chapel
15. Retrochoir
16. Chapel of the Purification or Chapel of the High Constable of Castile
17. St. James's Chapel
18. Sacristy
19. St. Henry's Chapel

20. Cloister Door
21. Chapel of the Visitation
22. Chapel of St. John of Sahagún
23. Chapel of the Relics
24. Chapel of the Presentation
25. Chapel of the Holy Christ of Burgos
26. Cloister
27. St. John the Baptist's Chapel
28. St. Catherine's Chapel
29. Corpus Christi Chapel

BURGOS AND ITS CATHEDRAL

THE HISTORICAL BACKGROUND

Despite modern development, the city of Burgos retains much of its medieval nucleus, with a noticeable mark left by the Gothic period. Born *ex novo* in the Middle Ages, it was to be the typical new Christian city, which would differentiate it clearly from others that had been previously conditioned by Roman settlements or Moslem peculiarities. Burgos was to develop especially during the late medieval period, leaving us much of its original layout and many buildings, outstanding among which is the Cathedral. The Cathedral is the major material and historical reference of the city, as well as the landmark announcing the presence of the city to travellers, whether pilgrims on their way to Santiago, medieval merchants, regal personages or the tourists of today.

Although there are remains of previous human settlement, the first written records concerning Burgos mention the foundation by Count Diego Porcelos in 884 AD of a fortress to form part, as one more bastion, of the system of Christian resistance to the Moslems in the territory north of the Douro (together with Amaya, Ubierna, Castrojeriz, etc.)

That fortification was the seed of a city which would start to develop as early as the Romanesque period of the 11th and 12th Centuries as a consequence of several favourable historical factors, both general and specific, including its situation at an important route centre and its political and ecclesiastical life.

An important factor in the city's development was the establishment of a diocesan see, considered the canonical successor to the ancient Visigothic bishopric of Oca. Great variation existed among the dioceses of the early Middle Ages as to jurisdiction, nature and seat, as a consequence of the weakness of settlement and changing frontiers, so there was nothing strange in the appearance of ephimeral bishoprics at Valpuesta, Muñó, Amaya or Sasamón, which would be absorbed into that of Oca on its restoration in the 11th Century within the new diocese of Burgos.

The monarchy favoured the new diocese, King Sancho II of Castile generously endowing its see in 1068. On the 8th July, 1074, the infantas (princesses) Doña Urraca and Doña Elvira donated the church of Gamonal to Don Jimeno, the Bishop of Burgos, in order for the seat of the diocese to be established in it. The process culminated with King Alfonso VI naming Burgos capital of the diocese and giving as an offering to it the palace which had belonged to Ferdinand I, together with the neighbouring Church of St Mary.

Preceding page: *Tambour and dome on the transept.*

One of the outstanding volumes of the external surface of the Cathedral is the tambour, built over the central section of the transept. After the collapse in 1539 of the tambour built in the 15th Century by John of Cologne, this impressive ensemble was built over the period 1539-68 by Juan de Vallejo. The artistic vocabulary is Renaissance, but the thoroughness of its use and the spaciousness are characteristic of the late Gothic period dominating the higher parts of the Cathedral. Apostles, saints, kings and other statues were sculpted by such qualified artists as Colindres, Picard, Andrés, Carranza and Castrillo, among others.

A detail of the pinnacles of the tambour. Enlivened with sculpture and decoration, with their weight these pinnacles confirm the safety of the construction and visually lighten its volume with the verticality they confer on it.

The city's episcopal status was further enhanced as the diocese of Burgos did not come under the Metropolitan of Toledo, Archbishop Bernard (1186-1224), who had been recognized by the Pope as primate of all the Kingdoms of Spain, when the Pontifice himself ruled that Burgos was "exempt" and to be administered directly from Rome (a situation which persisted until Burgos acquired the rank of Metropolitan Church in 1572).

Romanesque Burgos became very important, as is borne out by its numerous hospitals and churches, outstanding among which was the Cathedral of St. Mary. This was the Cathedral known to El Cid, who directed to it his last gaze on the way to exile, as the poems says: "He turned the horse's head towards St Mary's/Raised his right hand and made the sign of the Cross."

The development of Burgos, however, not only continued but increased, so much so that it was one of the most dynamic cities of the Gothic period, such radical renewal determining that practically nothing remains of the Romanesque city. From the beginning of the 13th Century until the dawn of the Renaissance, certain political, strategic, historical and mercantile factors afforded Burgos a period of splendour. And its symbol was to be the Cathedral, which reflected royal attention to the city, the growth of a merchant oligarchy and the presence of cultivated clergy, especially as regards prelates and chapter members.

The diocese of Burgos was, moreover, very large, as it included most of the modern province of the same name and reached the Cantabrian coast, taking in Santander and parts of what are now the provinces of La Rioja and Palencia. This contributed to the wealth of the heritage of the prelates and chapter members, who were able to fund different constructions and works of art in the Cathedral, nearly all initiatives coming from religious quarters, private donations being exceptions, though sometimes notable, as is the case of the Chapel of the High Constable of Castile.

Outside view, from the Northwest.

Detail of the right-hand tower, with the spiral staircase housing. There are three remarkable external volumes: the towers, the tambour in the centre and, at the back, the High Constable's Chapel. The architecture is enlivened with decorative motifs and especially with statues, which on the towers are of members of the royal family.

THE SETTING AND THE URBAN SURROUNDINGS

In order to understand the construction of the cathedral and the views of it in the city, we must take into account the nature of its site.

It has already been mentioned that the city of Burgos sprang from the Castle built on a hill dominating the area watered by the river Arlanzón. At first there would have been a small population on the hillside next to the castle, but in time it spread down onto the flat land by the river.

The Cathedral was erected between the hillside and the low-lying area, so there is a considerable difference in height between the old Coronería Street (now Fernán González Street), which runs along the north side of the Cathedral, and the Cathedral floor, and between the floor and Paloma Street, along the south side. Such topographical conditions imply certain characteristics which we shall come back to when we consider the doors, stairways, etc. of the church.

Apart from the streets mentioned, in the area surrounding the Cathedral there are several small squares offering different views of the outside of the building. Before the western gable end over St Mary's door lies the square of the same name. There was once a cemetery here, later a meat and fish market, which became a fruit market in the 13th Century. A substantial improvement was brought about by Bishop Pablo de Santamaría in about 1429 when Azogue Square was laid out with a fountain in the middle.

The square we have today is the fruit of later alterations, especially those made in 1663 by master stonemason Juan de Sierra, when several houses were

General view from the other side of the River Arlanzón

The silhouette of the Cathedral could easily be seen over the city wall (on a site now occupied by blocks of flats) and St Mary's Gate, which was embellished in the 16th Century with the statues of Burgos heroes and Emperor Charles V. Once inside the city gates, a good close-up view of the Cathedral may be enjoyed, as the old Archbishop's Palace, which was built onto it, was demolished at the beginning of the 20th Century.

pulled down, and the outside wall acquired the stairway up to St Nicholas and Fernán González Street. Those works also included a new fountain, for which Clemente de Quintana sculpted the Virgin, seraphim and other ornamentation.

On the southern side, between the city gate and the Cathedral lies San Fernando Square, a recent development affording good general views of the structure of the building from the southwest, especially since the demolishing in 1914 of the old Archbishop's Palace, which used to block views of this side of the Cathedral.

From a third square, open on the eastern side, we can contemplate the outside of the apse of the temple and the Chapel of the High Constable of Castile thanks to urban reforms of the late 19th Century, when several buildings that backed onto the Cathedral wall were cleared away, among them the *Casa de Obra*, a Cathedral workshop.

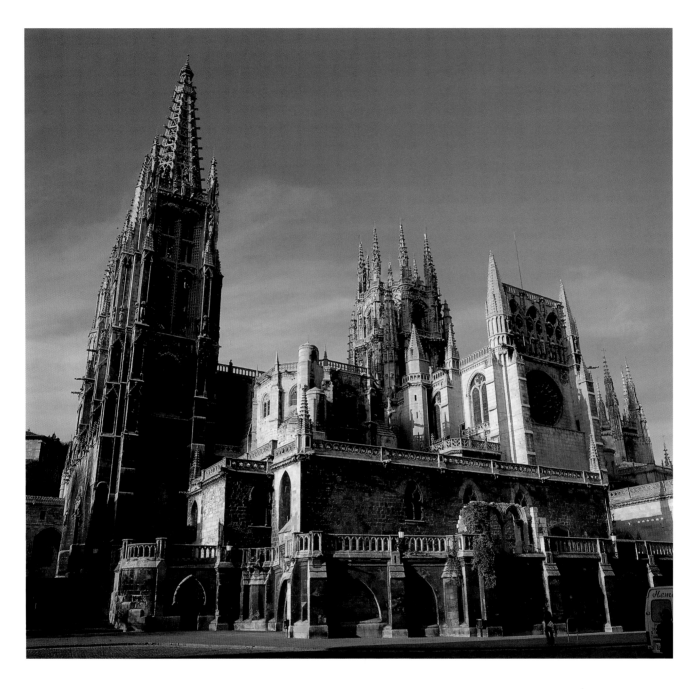

This square joins the atrium of the *Pellejería* door, which replaced the *Corralejo* (courtyard) in the first third of the 16th Century.

It is interesting to note that from the southern side, a good view is available of the cloister. As Paloma Street is rather narrow, in the daytime the lower pathway on this side is open as a pedestrian thoroughfare, with splendid views of the stories of the cloister and other details.

View from the south, from inside the City Wall.

THE BUILDING

THE FIRST STAGE OF THE GOTHIC CATHEDRAL

B y the end of the 12th Century the old Romanesque Cathedral had a chapter of thirty canons, which together with the rising importance of the city was to give rise to the need for a larger church, as is indicated by the foresight of Bishop Marino (1182-1200) who donated several neighbouring houses on condition that they should be demolished if the Cathedral was to be enlarged.

Historical dynamism, the strategic situation of the city on the road to Santiago, on a major trade route, changing artistic tastes in Europe and the presence in the city of certain notable personages were decisive factors leading to the construction of a new cathedral. In 1213, the bishopric of Burgos passed to Don Mauricio, a cultivated man educated in Paris, and a man of the king's trust, so much so that in 1219 Ferdinand III sent him as his royal envoy to make the plans for his marriage to Beatrice of Swabia, the ceremony taking place in the old Cathedral. Two years later, on the 20th July, 1221, the first stone of the Gothic Cathedral was laid in the presence of Ferdinand III and Bishop Mauricio. Royal encouragement was obviously important in its construction, as was the agreement of the Chapter, the diocese and the city of Burgos, but of especial importance was the wise direction of the prelate: "...the very wise Mauricio, Bishop of Burgos, built strong and beautiful the church of Burgos" (Lucas de Tuy).

The Cathedral was built in several stages, of which the most decisive was the first one, which lasted barely a century from 1221, the bulk of the construction being finished by the end of the 13th Century . Work must have gone on feverishly in the first part of this period, for in 1230, the choirmaster Pedro Díaz de Villahoz donated money for the completion of St Nicholas's Chapel, in the transept; eight years later Bishop Mauricio was buried in the presbytery, and in 1257 mention is made of the north face of the transept. So much progress was made that by the end of the 13th Century work was taking place on the cloisters, where in the first decades of he 14th Century, the eastern chapels were already going up.

The names of the artists who worked on the construction during the first hundred years are not known with any certainty. An initial participation by Master Ricardo, who had previously worked at Las Huelgas has been supposed, though other authors prefer to attribute the work to a more modern French craftsman. Mention is made in 1227 of a canon called Master Johan of Champagne and, although we do not know if in he actually played any artistic rôle, his name does sound suggestive in the Cathedral's early years. The first artisan whose name is known for certain is Master Enrique, active in the middle of the 13th Century, for mention is made of "Juan Anrric, the master craftsman's son..." Enrique was also

Silhouette at dusk of the spires on the High Constable's Chapel, the tambour and the towers.

Left: *Views of the Cathedral from the castle, and from St Mary's Arch, through winter mist.*

13

Spire on the right-hand tower of the Cathedral, finished in the 15th Century by John of Cologne at the behest of Bishop Alonso de Cartagena, whose shield, with its fleur de lys, and the king's flank the statue of Christ the Judge or the Man in Pain, who shows the wounds of His passion.

Right: *Romantic view of the High Constable's Chapel, according to an interpretation by David Roberts.*

to be the master craftsman of León Cathedral and when he died in 1277, the church calendar describes him as *magister operis burgensis ecclesiae*. Later work at Burgos was carried out by Master Johan Pérez (d. 1296), who was buried in the new Gothic cloister which he had helped to build. Other masons who took part in the work included Aparicio Pérez, in 1327, Pedro Sánchez de Molina (d. 1396) and Martín Fernández (d. 1418).

The groundplan of the Gothic Cathedral is a Latin cross measuring 84 metres by 59. There is a triple nave with each part divided into six sections, which are square in the aisles and crosswise rectangular in the wider nave. The transept is a single nave with three sections in each arm. The nave is projected into a deep apse with three rectangular sections and a semidecagonal end with an ambulatory round it. Off the ambulatory there are several chapels, most with later alterations. On the southeastern side of the church the Gothic cloister was built, the Romanesque cloister being maintained for a time in the southwest, where it was gradually encroached upon by episcopal palaces, chapels and other buildings. Some chapels were built off the aisles, but with difficulty, as the lie of the land cut them short on the north side, while the south side was already taken up by the buildings covering the old cloister.

Inside, we can see that the elevation of the Cathedral follows French patterns of the classical phase of the Gothic period, with cylindrical piers backed by ribs, which form the arches and the nerves of the vaults. The wall of the nave comprises three superimposed tiers of lights: the arches linking the nave with the aisles, an extensive - but not very deep - triforium extradosed with a wealth of human heads, and, thirdly, large pointed windows, which light up the inside. More light is admitted by a large rose window at the foot of the nave and another in the southern arm of the transept, the former in the shape of a star of David and the other with the circumference decorated with a tracery of trefoiled arches and an outer corona of small quatrefoil rosettes.

The original vaulting is of vaults with simple networks of ribs, to which a longitudinal tie has been added in the nave (the sections with more complex vaults belong to later reconstructions). There is a curious detail in the vault over the chancel, where small round windows lighten the cells between the ribs, a detail seen in French cathedrals such as Bourges and which was to spread throughout Castile (Grijalba, Aguilar de Campóo, the old cathedral of Valladolid, etc.) from Burgos.

Summing up, it can be said that Burgos Cathedral is the result of the use of a number of ideas from the French Classical Gothic style: the plan and the vaulting are reminiscent of the Coutances model, while the elevation shows a clearer link with Bourges, the double buttresses bring to mind the great churches of Saint Denis of Paris, and the organization of the façades is like that of Reims.

LATE MEDIEVAL AND SIXTEENTH CENTURY ALTERATIONS

Different historical circumstances brought great prosperity to Burgos in the closing decades of the middle ages, when the city achieved a notable economic and cultural preeminence, which was to continue into the 16th Century and is clearly reflected in work on the Cathedral, where a late Gothic stamp with Renaissance echoes is to be noticed.

These alterations to the Cathedral were permitted by several church dignitaries and by Burgos society. Among the prelates, special mention must be made of the strong personality of Don Alonso de Cartagena (1435-1456), an educated man and a prolific writer, thanks to whose efforts a new stage was initiated in the life of the Cathedral, as is reflected in the funerary chapel of the Visitation and the

spires erected on the towers or the old tambour, later rebuilt. We shall also remember Bishop Luis de Acuña (1457-1495), who completed the former's work on the Cathedral spires and built a fine funerary chapel dedicated to the Conception and St Anne, and Bishop Juan Rodríguez de Fonseca (1514-1525), promoter of the famous Golden Stairway and the Skinners' Door. To these prelates we may add certain members of the chapter, notably Canon Gonzalo de Lerma, who is responsible for the Chapel of the Presentation. Apart from the clergy, we must also remember the High Constable of Castile, who had the impressive Chapel of the Purification built off the centre of the Ambulatory.

By now the names of the craftsmen are known, pride of place going to the Cologne dynasty founded in the middle of the 15th Century by John of Cologne (or, Juan de Colonia), who was called in by Bishop Alonso de Cartagena to build the chapel, spires on the towers and the tambour. His son Simon of Cologne (or, Simón de Colonia) was to be more active, leaving behind him above all Bishop Acuña's and the High Constable's chapels. The third link in the family, Francisco de Colonia, born in the Renaissance, built the Skinners' Door and the High Constable's sacristy. Although employed at the time mainly as a sculptor, the young Diego de Siloe left the mark of his genius in the famous Golden Stairway. Other brilliant sculptors involved were the Gothic Gil de Siloe and the

Engraving (from España Sagrada - "Sacred Spain" - by E. Flórez, vol. XXVI) made in 1771 showing what the triple western door was like before it was altered owing to the deterioration of the stonework.

Renaissance Philippe de Bigarny, while in ironwork Cristóbal de Andino and many others are of note. In the second third of the 16th Century, several architects stand out, especially Juan de Vallejo, who was responsible for the rebuilding of the tambour after its collapse in 1539.

Top left and right: French-inspired system of buttresses and double flying buttresses, which strengthen the building and carry rainwater away down channels and through gargoyles.

MODERN CONTRIBUTIONS

Few later alterations were made to the Cathedral, although in the second half of the 16th Century, Gothic vaulting is abandoned for the Chapel of the Nativity, erected off the ambulatory by Martín de Bérriz and Martín de la Haya.

Among the most important Baroque additions is the enclosing of the choir funded by Archbishop Antonio Zapata (1599-1604), whose munificence continued after he left to become a cardinal. The classicism of this work is echoed later in St Henry's Chapel, built by Archbishop Enrique de Peralta y Cárdenas. But the Baroque style comes into its own in the Chapel of St Tecla, promoted in 1731-36 by Archbishop Manuel de Samaniego (1728-1741), its heavy ornamentation being repeated some years later in the sacristy and Chapel of the Relics.

Later works are mainly concerned with consolidation and restoring the Cathedral, among which those started at the beginning of the 19th Century by Vicente Lampérez and finished by Apraiz, and modern repairs made by Marcos Rico since 1975, are worthy of note.

THE OUTSIDE

T he outside of the temple is the result of different artistic contributions, although in the main the structure belongs to the 13th Century, to the Gothic period, when the nave and aisles, the west face, the façade of the transept, the cloister and several of the chapels were built. Some later works have been built onto this nucleus, especially the spires atop the towers at the corners, the tambour over the centre of the transept and the high-ceilinged Chapel of the High Constable in the apse, other later works being much less significant.

THE WEST FACE: THE ROYAL DOOR, DOOR OF PARDON OR ST MARY'S DOOR

West face.

An attractive 13th Century construction onto whose towers John of Cologne added Swabo-German spires in the mid-15th Century. The lower triple door is easily noticed as the result of late 18th Century alterations, carried out owing to deterioration of the original Gothic stonework.

The west face is the most monumental, as it was the most important, being surmounted by two towers built over the first section of the aisles.

From the correct viewpoint we should concentrate now on the towers and high parts. Here, as in other parts of the outside of the Cathedral, various sculptures were arranged with the singular ideological purpose of associating things sacred with the Castellano-Leonese monarchy, in a way somewhat reminiscent of the French Cathedral of Chartres. Thus we can see the eight monarchs of Castile-León from Ferdinand I to Alfonso IX, Ferdinand III's father. Others have also been identified, such as Henry I, Doña Berenguela and, on the right-hand tower, the seven sons of Ferdinand III.

The high part of the central body and the two slender spires were added in the middle of the 15th Century by John of Cologne. In the centre is an outstanding sculpture of the Virgin, with an inscription in Gothic letters reading *pulchra es et decora* on the plinth. The two openwork spires crowning the towers are inspired by Swabo-German models and it is considered very likely that the artist was familiar with the project for the towers of Cologne cathedral, which had already been designed but were not to be erected until the 19th Century. John of Cologne put parapets on the square 13th Century towers to ease the transition to the octagonal bases of the spires: on one of them we can see the legend *pax vobis* and a sculp-

Top and Bottom: *Details of the triple western door, where in 1805 these statues were placed. Some are said to be of King Alfonso VI and Bishop Simón, promoters of the Romanesque Cathedral. The others are of Ferdinand III and Bishop Mauricio, instigators of the Gothic construction.*

Right: *The second story of the west face has a large rose window with tracery of quatrefoil circles surrounding a star of David admitting light into the nave. Above it there is an elegant arcade with statues of royal personages, based on the French idea at Chartres. The ensemble is crowned with a balustrade and a Gothic inscription dedicated to the Virgin.*

ture of the Christ of the Pains, and on the other, *ecce agnus dei* and St John the Baptist, together with several shields of the monarchy and of Bishop Alonso de Cartagena, who funded the work. At the top of each spire is a circular gangway with the Gothic monograms IHS and SM on the railings together with the arms of the prelate Luis de Acuña, who saw the work finished. Literary evidence exists, however, to suggest that the towers culminated in statues of St Peter and St Paul, perhaps removed for reasons of safety.

In the lower part of the face a triple doorway opens onto the nave and aisles. It is called the Royal Door, for, as a document written in 1257 tells us, it was the "main door of the Church used by the King and Queen in processions". Alternative names are St Mary's Door and the Door of Pardon. The original doorway has disappeared owing to deterioration of the stonework, although we have knowledge of it from the literature and from an old engraving published in a work by Enrique Flórez in 1771. As it was triple and opened onto the nave and aisles it was the most monumental of the cathedral's portals. The central opening, the widest, was surmounted by a tympanum with several superimposed tiers, with the Death of the Virgin and above it the Trinity, and the doorway itself was divided by a great mullion with "an image, lovelier than reality, of the Holy Virgin" according to Friar Bernardo Palacios writing in 1729.

It was, then, a characteristic doorway of the early stages of Castilian Gothic, with the Marian imagery repeated throughout the 13th Century in the region, examples being the cathedrals of Ciudad Rodrigo, Burgo de Osma and León.

The deterioration of the carved stonework caused the side doorways to be altered as early as 1663, when Juan de Pobes sculpted above them the reliefs of the Conception and the Assumption, replacing the original tympana. The condition of the stonework got so bad that in 1753 and 1768, several blocks had to be dismantled, leaving the reliefs and the image of the Virgin on the mullion of the central doorway unrecognizable. It was then that the member of the Academy of San Fernando Don Alfonso Regalado Rodríguez proposed the atrium should be altered and a new doorway built, with a lintel and no mullion, the idea being accepted by the Cathedral and its architect Fernando González de Lara. Thus in 1790, the classicist doorway we know today was built. Four statues were added in 1805: Don Asterio and Alfonso VI (respectively the Bishop of Oca in 589 and the king who created the diocese of Burgos) on one side, and Ferdinand III and Don Mauricio (the promoters of the Gothic Cathedral) on the other. The side doorways were contributed by Juan de Pobes in the 17th Century, with reliefs in their lancet-shaped tympana and an oval window over the lintelled doorway. The one on the right is dedicated to the Immaculate Conception, a subject which does not belong to the Gothic style but which does belong to the 17th Century, when the work was done, with the Virgin trampling on the dragon on a crescent, surrounded by allegories of Marian litanies (a tower, gilded house, orchard, well, mirror, etc.) and angels crowning her. The left-hand tympanum is dedicated to the Assumption of Mary, who is carried up through clouds by angels holding her mantle, while another two play string instruments and two more place a crown on her head.

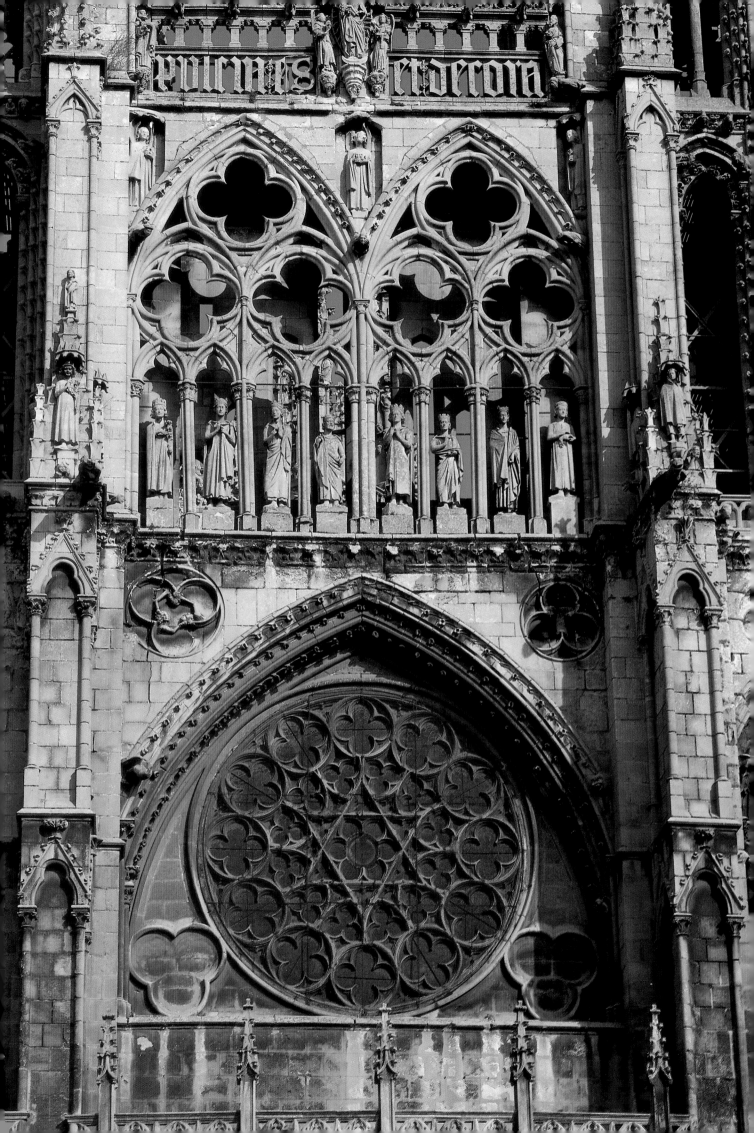

THE SOUTH FACE: THE *SARMENTAL* DOOR

A walk around the outside of the Cathedral might begin on the south side, at San Fernando Square, where in the foreground a flight of steps goes up to the *Sarmental* Door. To its left is the space occupied until the beginning of the 20th Century by the bishop's palace, laid out next to the Old Cloister, which was built over part of the old Romanesque site. On the right, a wall encloses the Gothic cloister, which has two stories and a lower pathway used as a pedestrian thoroughfare to take part of the burden off narrow Paloma Street. Without going any further forward to get a better view, one can observe the tambour over the centre of the cathedral rebuilt in the middle of the 16th Century by Juan de Vallejo after the collapse of John of Cologne's work of the previous century. Although its details are Renaissance, one can still detect a late Gothic feeling in the morphology, windows and pinnacles. On its southern side there stands silhouetted an equestrian statue of St James, most fitting for such an important landmark on the way to Santiago.

Projecting from this face is the gable end of the arm of the transept, the structure of which is conditioned by its having only one nave. From afar we can appreciate a tripartite vertical division: the doorway, above which there is a rose window giving light to the inside, the finishing touch being an animated tracery arcade framing a wealth of statuary.

Here, statues depict a scene considered to be the "Divine Liturgy", a subject of Byzantine origin where the Christ of the Eucharist is surrounded by angels bearing censers and candles.

Below that is the *Sarmental* Door, the oldest door of the Cathedral. The scene is dominated by the tympanum, with the Maiestas of Christ, enthroned and crowned and accompanied by the Tetramorph and the figures of the same evangelists writing at their desks. The iconography is old-fashioned for its time, being more normal for previous periods, which means that it could be a repetition of something from the Romanesque Cathedral or simply the will of the churchmen who decided on the themes to be depicted. Although the subject is traditional, its execution is innovatory, as it must have been carried out by a master craftsman of French quality and classical ideals, as he has been identified with the "master of the Beau Dieu of Amiens". In the same artistic line of Gothic Classicism, in the apostles set on the lintel of the door, a greater naturalism is evident, with varied postures, a degree of animation and feet set outside the border, although the sculptor is thought to have been of the French school owing to the purity and substantial expressiveness of the images. Moreover, we must consider the corbels supporting the lintel, one of which portrays the classical theme of the "thorn" (a young man taking a thorn out of his foot). The imagery on the archivolts maintains a certain archaism with the set of apocalyptic old men and choirs of angels, though the outer arches do have modern subjects, about which a hypothesis has been formed concerning an interpretation of the allegory of the Arts, as may also be seen in the Cathedral of Chartres: the music of the Quadrivium would be symbolized by people playing an organ or bells, and the Trivium would include Grammar, where children would be depicted with a book and another child bent on reading; Geometry shows a table and two children, one of whom has a pair of compasses, while Medicine appears as a seated personage examining a container.

The mullion in the doorway carries a canopy with the Lamb of God, who shelters an impressive statue of a bishop traditionally considered to be Don Mauricio, the founder of the Gothic Cathedral. However, this does not seem likely, as it would not have been fitting to place a statue of the prelate in such a prominent place during his lifetime. It is therefore better to think of it as one of the ancient prelates or one of saintly repute of the early days of the diocese of Burgos. So, as an argument of historical anthority, the statue may have been

Top: *Aaron with a censer , and another personage on the left-hand jamb.*

The Sarmental *Door constitutes an important ensemble of sculpture, dating from about 1230, where French masters worked together with Spanish associates. The statues on the jambs are later. The statue on the mullion is especially remarkable, and is traditionally supposed to be the instigator of the Gothic Cathedral and of this door, but is more probably Don Asterio, Bishop in 589 of the Visigothic see of Oca, from which that of Burgos arose in the 11th Century.*

Left: *The* Sarmental *Door.*

Bottom: *Capital of the* Sarmental *Door. It represents the Deesis, the Virgin and St John interceding before Christ the Judge, a subject repeated on the* Coronería *Door.*

Details of the Sarmental *Door.*

There is remarkable artistic quality with beauty and realism. Christ in Majesty, with a crown and nimbus in the background, is surrounded by the evangelists and their symbols, the Tetramorph. In the lower part, the apostles are engaged in sacred conversation, with notable naturalism.

Other details are also interesting: at the top, the corbels under the lintel show a man reading and another removing a thorn from his foot. (The Thorn is a classic sculpture subject.)

intended as a portrayal of Don Asterio, who, in the year 589 , was Bishop of the Visigothic see of Oca, the foreunner of the Burgos diocese. It is less likely to be St. Indalecio, the legendary evangelizer of the Oca region, as no medieval record of his Cathedral worship exists.

On the door jambs there are several sculptures of St Peter, St Paul, Moses, Aaron and others, which are later than the door itself. Furthermore, iconographic reasons compel us to judge two of the capitals of the jambs. One of them, on the left, represents the Deesis, with Christ the judge in the centre showing his wounds, accompanied by two angels with instruments of passion, together with the Virgin and St John interceding on the behalf of humanity (a subject which precedes that of the Crowning and which was to be widely echoed in the Gothic sculpture of the region). The other capital, on the right, shows the ancient scene of the Knight.

Left: *Detail of the "Divine Liturgy" scupture group.*

Rose window and top of the Sarmental Face

Over the door there is a large rose window giving light to the single nave of the transept, and above this is an open arcade concealing the roofing and adorned by the "Divine Liturgy" sculpture group, with Jesus officiating accompanied by angels carrying candles and censers.

27

THE NORTH FACE:
THE APOSTLES' DOOR, OR *CORONERIA* DOOR

From St Mary's Square, at the feet of the church, access to the northern part of the outside of the Cathedral is afforded by a long flight of steps leading up to Fernán González Street, in times gone by known as *Corronería, Correría, Cornería* and *Coronería* Street, perhaps because leather workers lived there, as in Vitoria. In 1257, the presence of Gutierre the *Correonero's* house is mentioned there.

It was a very busy street in the middle ages, used both by city traffic and by commercial traffic on the Santiago road crossing the city between St John's Gate, in the northeast, and St Martin's Gate in the southwest.

The outer walls of the Chapels of St Tecla and St Anne back onto this street. While these are of no special artistic interest, the same cannot be said of the little chapel built onto them dedicated to the Virgin of Joy, to whom even today a devote public keeps a candle permanently lit. The image is a beautiful Gothic one of the Virgin and Child mentioned at least as early as 1479 in Cathedral documents. The sculpture is typical of the third quarter of the 13th Century and is a seated, full-face Virgin with the Child already moving His right leg, which He rests on His Mother's mantle.

The most important part of this north face is the Apostles' Door, by which name it was known as early as 1257, although owing to its position, it was also to become known as the *Coronería* Door. It must have been made about 1250, with a Hispanicized expressiveness which was more naturalistic than that of the *Sarmental* Door, although its artists would have acquired their skills in the Gothic movement under the masters working on the *Sarmental* Door. Its maker is known as the "master of the *Coronería*", and is thought to have belonged to Master Enrique's workshop.

It has the shape of a pointed arch, with archivolts and sculptures on the jambs, but it must have been altered at the end of the 16th Century, when the mullion was removed and the doorway was strengthened with Mannerist architecture.

The iconography of this door is clearly Gothic and is associated with models at Reims Cathedral. Most notable is the tympanum, divided into a lower strip and a higher area. In this upper part is the seated figure of Christ the Judge, in the centre of the piece, showing the wounds of his passion and accompanied by the Virgin and St John, who implore for mankind, while angels bear the *arma Christi* (instruments of his Passion: a spear, column, cross, nails, crown of thorns). It is an example of the *Deesis* a theme repeated with variants in the eastern Christian world, and which in the west takes on this version. After Burgos, it was to be repeated, as has already been said, in other buildings in the region.

The lower strip of the tympanum bears a theme derived from the Judgement in the upper part, the Psychostasy, or weighing of the souls of the dead by St Michael, who is depicted in the centre, separating to one side the damned, who are dragged away by demons, while on the other side is an angel who has taken the soul of someone saved, whose destiny it is to pass through the Gates of Heaven, behind which serenely stand the blessed, friars and kings, among whom one tradition identifies St Dominic and St Francis showing the papal bulls of their respective orders to King Ferdinand III and Bishop Mauricio.

The subject of the saved and the damned continues outside the tympanum onto the ower sculptures on the archivolts, where on the right are shown tortures and condemned souls burning in the furnace, while the left-hand part bears angels welcoming the souls of the blessed. Likewise, the outer archivolt shows various scenes of the resurrection of the dead. The other two archivolts are taken up by angels: cherubim on the inner part and angels bearing candles and censers on the middle part.

Coronería *Door, or Apostles' Door*

So called because of the old name of the street and the set of sculptures adorning its jambs, it is dedicated to the Day of Judgement, with Christ the Judge on the tympanum and the resurrection of the dead on the archivolts while, on the lintel, St Michael weighs souls, separating the blessed from the damned, who are punished by demons. The late-16th Century Mannerist framework reduces the doorway.

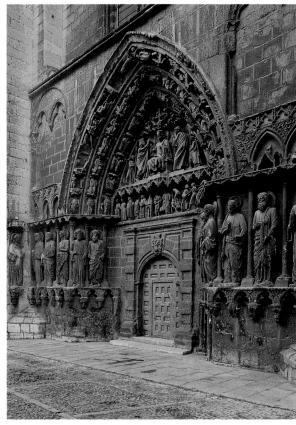

The *Coronería* Door was known from earliest times as the Apostles' Door, for as at Chartres cathedral, its wide jambs carry a set of sculptures of the Apostles. They would appear to be the work of an artist of quality and influenced by French styles of expression. The six sculptures on each side are difficult to identify, except in certain cases, like St Andrew. Their heads are fairly similar, though the composition and treatment of the bodies divides them into two groups. Six are given vertical folds in their garments, which lends them a hieratic aspect, offset by the width of their cuffs, while the other six have their mantles draped diagonally, giving animation and variety to the imagery.

Above the door, the northern gable end is organized somewhat differently from the southern one, above the *Sarmental* Door, as the lie of the land leaves it less space. So, instead of a large rose window, there is a simple triple Gothic window, protected by a fine frieze picked out with three little heads. It does, however, culminate in a structure of openwork arches surrounding statues of personages connected with the monarchy, in agreement with the ideological exaltation, as at Chartres, which seeks to associate divine concepts with Castilian royalty.

Details of the Coronería *Door*

Christ the Judge displays the wounds of His passion, the instruments of which ("arma Christi") are born by angels. As in the Byzantine Deesis, the Virgin and St John - here the beloved disciple - intercede on behalf of humanity. The left-hand side of the archivolts bears the resurrection of the dead, angels with candles and censers, and cherubim.

THE APSE OF THE CATHEDRAL:
THE *PELLEJERÍA* (SKINNERS') DOOR

Today this part gives onto an open space known as the Llana de Afuera (Outer Plain) where there used to be a building of the Sea Consulate, and which was also occupied by houses and the Cathedral workshops. Here we can see the outsides of the chapels built off the ambulatory, as well as a side door more accessible from the inside than the Apostles' Door.

The Skinners' Door opens to one side of the northern arm of the transept, as an exit to an old Courtyard once situated next to the apse. It was where the cathedral workshop used to be, so it was necessary for the easy access of workmen, as well as for the residents of the Skinners' Quarter and San Llorente Street (now Fernán González Street), from which a flight of steps was built reaching down to this door. The steps and the door, assigned to John of Cologne, form part of a set of alterations instigated by the educated Renaissance prelate Juan Rodríguez de Fonseca. The Skinners' Door was begun by the representative of the third generation of the Colonia dynasty, Francisco de Colonia, who lacked his forebears' genius, as may be noticed in the forced adaptation of shapes and decoration to Renaissance innovations.

The Skinners' Door is organized as a triumphal arch flanked by bodies with vertical recesses containing statues of St James, St Andrew, and the two St Johns - the Baptist and the Apostle - patrons of the instigator of the work. Pilasters, columns and frieze are illustrated with fine Renaissance decoration of grotesque forms copied from the work of the Milanese Friar Antonio de Monza and other artists. Over the door, with similar ornamentation, there are two reliefs concerning the martyrdom of St John the Baptist and St John the Apostle, which still retain the background of scales typical of the Colonias' school, as is also to be seen in the relief crowning this doorway, a semicircle framing Bishop Rodríguez de Fonseca kneeling before the Virgin and Child, with three angel musicians flanked by effigies of St Peter and St Paul. Some details betray a certain overdone late Gothic, notably the existence of an archivolt with small sculptures around the round arch of the door. Also present is the repetition of crests, typical of the time, including several shields of the Cathedral (the vase of Madonna lilies) and of the prelate (the five stars of the Fonseca family).

Here we can appreciate the architectural morphology of some of the Gothic chapels of the ambulatory. However the monumentality of the High Constable's Chapel overshadows the others in the centre of the ambulatory. To be admired is the slender elegance of the architecture, which from a polygonal groundplan thrusts Heavenwards a volume pierced by windows and rendered more graceful by the spires typical of the end of the 15th Century, when Simon of Cologne built this chapel for the first High Constable and his wife. Notice should be taken of the sculpture work used by these stalwarts to record their funding of this funeral chapel. Supporters bear monumental shields of the surnames of Pedro Fernández de Velasco and Mencía de Mendoza y Figueroa, the former with the vair of the Velascos, an orle charged with castles and lions, while the latter is quartered with the arms of the Mendozas (party per saltire with the inscription AVE MARIA) and Figueroas (fig leaves). Likewise included are the favourite emblems of the family of the High Constable, such as St Andrew's cross, the potency cross of Jerusalem and the monogram of the name of Jesus (IHS), brought into widespread use in the second half of the 15th Century by devotion to St Bernard.

Detail of the outside of the High Constable's Chapel

The importance of the founders of the chapel, the Velascos and the Mendozas, is made patent by the heraldry, for example this shield, with the checky and vair patterns proper to the surname Velasco, flanked by supporting pages. Furthermore, in the lower window there are two small insignias much favoured by the family: the monogram IHS and the cross potenty.

Left: Pellejería *Door*

Giving access from the Plain to the left arm of the transept, it was made on the initiative of the educated prelate Juan Rodríguez de Fonseca after 1515, with work by John of Cologne. It is a Renaissance piece with Grotesque motifs dedicated to St John the Evangelist and St John the Baptist, patron saints of the promoter, the arms of whose surname - five stars - are set on shields, as is the Marianist vase of Madonna lilies.

ART INSIDE

Inside the Cathedral: the nave

The great wealth of artwork accumulated inside the Cathedral has changed its appearance. From the choir, in the nave one may appreciate the Gothic architecture of the presbytery section, with a correct ribbed vault with a longitudinal rib, the sides of the vault being pierced with round windows. The transept shows its reconstruction of the mid 16th Century, which led to the placing of curved nerves in the nearest sections.

Different cathedrals are characterized by peculiar details (predominance of glass, space, and architectural or other features). In the case of Burgos, a great harmony is to be observed between its architectural value - it is the first important milestone in Spanish Gothic cathedral building - and the wealth of works of art that it has collected down the ages. These include architectural innovations such as some of the funerary chapels, preeminent among which is that of the High Constable. There is also a set of medieval and Renaissance tombs, which, starting with Don Mauricio's, include beautiful Gothic examples of diverse types and with different sculptural themes, and the Renaissance ones worked by Diego de Siloe or Philippe de Bigarny. The interior is also embellished by certain items of furniture, such as the choirstalls, the great reredos behind the High Altar and other Gothic, Renaissance and Baroque altarpieces in the chapels of especial expressive or iconographic significance.

Hispano-Flemish, Renaissance and Baroque paintings; silverware of great artistic value; Flemish and Hispanic tapestries, contribute together with other works of art to make Burgos Cathedral one of the richest.

There are many possible itineraries for a visit to the Cathedral, so here we shall set things out in such a way that the visitor may make up his own mind, referring to the book according to marked sections. First we shall concentrate on the nave and choir area, working apsewards from the choirstalls to the reredos of the High Altar. We shall then move on to the chapels or elements of artistry arranged around the temple, starting from the back of the northern aisle of the nave, and continuing to the northern arm of the transept, this side of the ambulatory, the southern arm of the transept and right-hand aisle to finish in the Chapel of the Christ of Burgos. We shall end with some of the works to be admired in the Cloister and the Museum inside it.

Before we go on, it must be made clear that the commentaries will be of a historical-artistic nature, with remarks concerning sponsorship, iconography, expressiveness, etc. but also that the main reason for art in a cathedral was specifically religious, cultural or liturgic, although we may now perceive its ideological and historical aspects.

The "Flycatcher" and "Little Martin" chime the quarters and strike the hours of the Cathedral clock.

The Nave

Looking from the feet of the Cathedral, first we should consider its very architecture, belonging to the classical Gothic period, with a notable eurhythmy of pillars, arches, triforium and windows. A set of heads enlivens the triforium, the tracery of which is noticeably different nearer the transept, as it was ruined here in the 16th Century and so is of the curved sort typical of the time of its reconstruction. The same may be said of the vault of the nave, of ribbed construction with a longitudinal rib reaching into the apse, but also with different tracery in the sections adjoining the transept for the same reason.

It is impossible to appreciate the original spaciousness as the view is obscured by the choir set in the middle of the nave during the 16th Century - common in Spanish cathedrals - the retrochoir being built in the 17th Century.

THE "FLYCATCHER"

Although it is not part of what is strictly speaking the artistic content of the building, it is impossible to miss, in the high part of the cathedral, in a window in the left-hand wall of the nave, a clock known popularly as the "Flycatcher", a clockwork artefact comprising several elements and which is more than just a timepiece. On a bracket on the neighbouring wall stands a character called Martinillo (Little Martin), ready to strike the quarters on two bells, while above the clock, looking out from the rose culminating the window is the figure of a man with a roguish face that opens its mouth once for each strike of the full hours.

We do not know the date of the manufacture of the Flycatcher, which is related to other mechanical and clockwork devices common in Central Europe and known in other parts of Spain, for example the Flycatcher in Palencia Cathedral or the *Mayorga* of Plasencia City Hall. The presence of the clock, however was important to mark the sequence of liturgical time, affecting also the life of the city. There is mention in the Cathedral records of the attention given to the clock as early as the 14th Century, while at the end of the 15th Century, foreigners are known to have been called in to attend to it, like Fadrique Alemán the printer or Juan de Norbárquer. References from the beginning of the 16th Century concern the addition of different religious or popular figures to the mechanism, and in the 17th repairs were made to the Flycatcher and to Martinillo, which were gone over again in 1743 by Francisco Alvarez, clockmaker to the Cathedral of Salamanca.

THE CHAPTER CHOIR

In the middle ages, Gothic choirstalls were set out in the chancel, as was usual in liturgy, maximum use thus being made of the deep presbytery of the chancel. Records show that it became too small for the number of choristers, and that certain dignatories did not have marked places, which is why the merchant Diego Pardo paid for a number of new stalls in 1467, while a further enlargement was considered in 1488. At the end of the 15th Century, the radical decision was taken to completely change the space used by the choir, involving the enclosing of the area behind screens to be made in 1499 by Master Bugil. By then, Philippe de Bigarny was working in the Cathedral, and his style caused a great impression of novelty at that time of great artistic changes, which means that it was not at all surprising that he should contribute to the Chapter's decision to renew the choirstalls.

Detail of the triforia along the sides of the nave.

This section, adjoining the transept, was reconstructed in the mid 16th Century.

Archbishop's Throne: details.

The archbishop's throne was made by the joiner Luis Gabeo and the carver García de Arredondo in the years 1583-87. One's attention is drawn by the presence together with the religious subjects of the Prayer in the Garden and the Tree of Jesse, of the mythological Rape of Europa.

partially gilded and has some enamelling on the pillow, maniple and upper part of the mitre. It is a noteworthy example normally attributed to the workshops of Limoges in the third quarter of the 13th Century, and Juaristi is of the opinion that it may have been made by Master John of Limoges around 1260.

Another remarkable piece in the choral area is the little statue of the Virgin on the Lectern, which is the work of the sculptor from Azpeitia Juan de Anchieta, an artist who worked on the main altarpiece in Burgos Cathedral and on another at the Monastery of Las Huelgas. It represents the Assumption in accordance with a composite formula repeated among Mannerist sculptors in the last third of the 16th Century, with an attitude of *contraposto* and a certain softness of forms.

As is normal for choirs, above the stalls there are two organs, which were used over a long period in worship and Cathedral liturgy. The one on the right is Baroque and is recorded as having been made by Master Juan de Argüeta in 1636 and altered at the beginning of the 18th Century by José de Echevarría. The organ on the left was made in 1806 and is the work of the master organ-maker Juan Manuel de Betolaza. Its console, by the joiner Manuel Cortés, is neo-Classical.

The enclosure of the choir area was carried out at the beginning of the 17th Century at the behest and under the sponsorship of the Burgos prelate Cardinal Antonio Zapata, an educated and well-connected man who had managed to bring Giambattista Crescenzi over from Italy, which permitted the artistic works of the Spanish court circle to take their place in the classicism of the Italian Baroque. In Burgos cathedral, Cardinal Zapata had the back of the choir area closed off to create an atmosphere of intimacy for the chapter. As well as funding the necessary seating, he had the work of the retrochoir done and had the front of the choir protected with a screen.

Top: *Transept, seen from the north.*

Right: *Nave, seen from the Chancel.*

The walls of the Cathedral are lightened by stories of arches, a large triforium and other windows, to which are added the large rose windows of the southern and western gable ends. The sobriety of the 13th-Century vaults is interrupted by the ornateness of the tambour and the neighbouring sections of the roof, typical of the mid 16th Century, when it was reconstructed.

Translator's note: ** Arcosolium: a decorative arch built against a wall, usually over a tomb.*

The Choir Screen is monumental, forming a membrane between the two great pillars of the transept. It was entrusted to Juan Bautista Celma, one of the most prolific and famous masters of his art within late Renaissance Mannerism, and priced in 1602 by Juan de Arfe. It was designed by the Valladolid painter Gregorio Martínez, who also took part in the execution of the main reredos, but when work was going on on the second body of the screen, it was altered in accordance with a new project drawn up by Celma himself, under Arfe's supervision. It stands on a plinth of jasper, with access at the sides. Atop two bodies of balusters is a group sculpture of Calvary, flanked by two shields, with the arms of the Cathedral (a vase of Madonna lilies) and of the funder of the screen, Archbishop Zapata (shoes).

Although Antonio Zapata left the diocese on being promoted to cardinal towards the end of 1604, he continued to sponsor the rear enclosing of the choir area from his see at Toledo. The work on the retrochoir, in accordance with this man's sensitivity and his court and artistic connections, was carried out with Classicist architecture using fine materials. To this effect, several artists were asked for projects, the choice being confided in the criterion of the active Carmelite architect Friar Alberto de la Madre de Dios, who selected the sketches presented by the architects Juan de Naveda and Felipe Alvaredo. The design incorporates a triumphal arch, with a wide central *arcosolium** intended to frame a painting, a pair of classical columns at each side with their intercolumns forming recesses for statues, at the foot of each of which is Cardinal Zapata's shield. In 1626, a fine canvas was hung in the centre depicting St Paul the hermit receiving the visit of St Anthony the Abbot (patron saint of the Cathedral), the picture having been sent from Madrid. In the side niches Classicist sculptures of St Peter

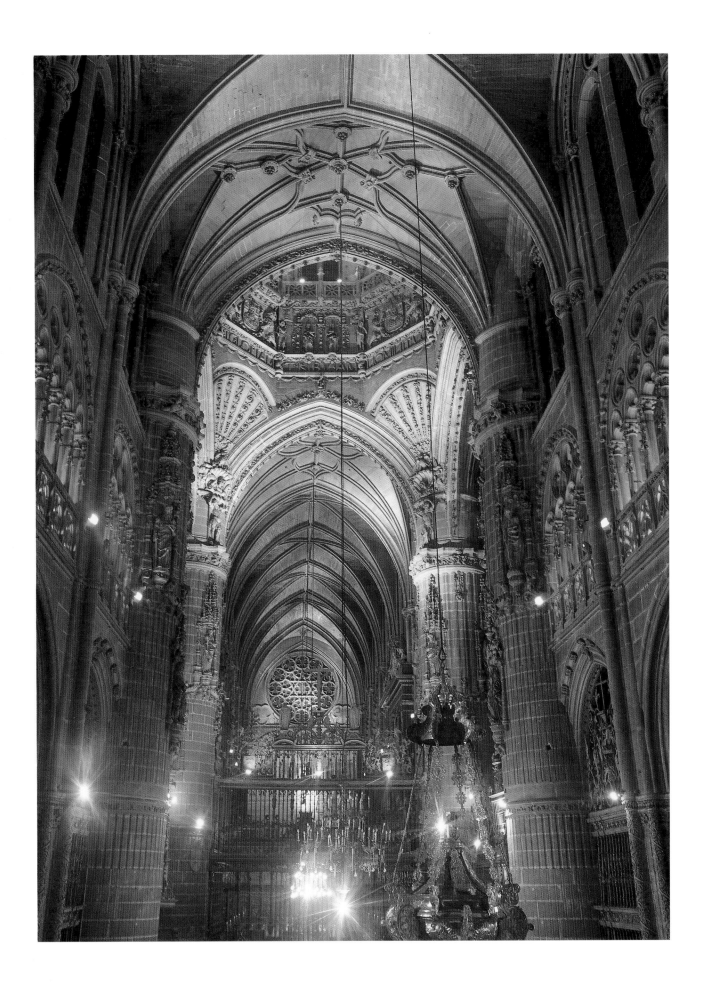

and St Paul were placed. Made of alabaster from Aleas (Cogolludo), they were ordered in 1623 from Antonio Riera, who worked under the supervision of the court architect Giambattista Crescenzi, whom we have already identified as a being of the Sponsor's trust.

Some years later, in the middle of the 17th Century, the work on the side enclosures was finished, the work having been started by Archbishop Francisco Manso de Zúñiga. For this work, the architect Juan de la Sierra drew up a project to bring it into harmony with previous work done on the retrochoir. The task was carried out over the period 1656-59 by Master Juan de los Helgueros. In the set of six recesses - three on either side - six canvasses by the Benedictine Friar were hung, with subjects concerning St Francis, patron saint of the incumbent prelate Manso de Zúñiga, St Anthony of Padua and saints especially related to the religious life of the diocese, such as St Centola, St Elena, St Julian, St Victoria and St Casilda.

THE TRANSEPT

Continuing from the choir down the nave past the screen protecting the stalls, we reach the centre of the cathedral, the intersection of the nave with the transept.

Here the visitor is overwhelmed by the tambour, which was rebuilt in the 16th Century. Let us not forget that in 1465, Master John of Cologne was working on a tambour of superb late Gothic beauty, surrounded by eight little towers, which caved in on the night of the 3rd-4th March, 1539, affecting the neighbouring sections of the vaults. That very day, the chapter set on foot the preparations for rebuilding the tambour and repairing what its fall had destroyed, in which they received the collaboration of different members of the religious, social and political life of the city.

The new tambour was begun in 1539, but was not finished until 1568, owing to the great wealth of sculptures used in its decoration and certain incidents that caused delays. We do not know who built it, although such men as Philippe de Bigarny and John of Langres are thought to have presented plans. At first, Juan de Vallejo and Francisco de Colonia worked together on the project, but after the latter's death, in 1542, Juan de Vallejo must have been the only master craftsman engaged on it until its conclusion.

The tambour was set on four great cylindrical piers, which allowed for an exceptionally tall structure in several tiers culminating in a ribbed vault with the ribs forming eight-pointed stars, and openwork inter-rib spaces, affording a zenithal luminosity completed by that of the windows and tinted by the stained glass made by Juan de Arce before 1573.

The work is decorated with a thoroughness typical of the late Gothic, although its vocabulary is Renaissance, as was preceptive at the time. Such sculptors as Colindres, Picardo, Carranza, and Castrillo are mentioned in the accounts paid for the sculptures and the reliefs in the tambour. In the lower part there are effigies of saints revered in the diocese, like St Centola, St Elena or St Victoria, and the Virgin in a composition blending the Immaculate Conception, the Assumption and the Coronation. Furthermore, between standard-bearing angels with the vase of Madonna lilies, the emblem of St Mary's Cathedral, there are several shields reflecting the effort made for the reconstruction of the tambour, among them the double-headed Eagle of Emperor Charles V, the arms of Archbishop Juan Alvarez of Toledo and those of the City of Burgos. A curious detail impossible to see from the Cathedral floor is to be found in the city arms, supported by lions, where there is a relief of the city, protected by walls with the houses and the Cathedral standing out and above, a phylactery with the inscription "INSINIA CIVITATIS".

In the upper part of the tambour there are several stone sculptures of prophets worked by Juan Picard and his son-in-law Pero Andrés, the creators of another set

The Tambour, over the transept.

The height of the centre of the Cathedral is truly impressive, with its high cylindrical piers bearing the windows and the vaulting.

Right: Vault of the tambour.

The ample openwork structure of the vault is overwhelming.

of outdoor statues on the high parts of the church, especially an equestrian St James dominating the southern part that Picard is on record as having made.

The visitor is standing in the centre of the transept, where the floor houses the Tomb of El Cid and his wife Doña Jimena, their remains having been brought here from the nearby Monastery of St Peter of Cardeña in 1921. The tomb is a simple block of marble bearing an inscription written by the illustrious philologist Ramón Menéndez Pidal at the time of the move.

Two side screens protect the access to the central section of the transept, funded by Archbishop Manuel Francisco Navarrete at the beginning of the 17th Century. It is known that they were drawn and the work directed by master architect Friar Pedro Martínez, a Benedictine monk from Cardeña, who also designed the adjoining pulpits. The screens, of especial interest for being made of bronze, were finished in 1718, perhaps by Basque grille makers, who were then at the forefront of this art.

THE CHANCEL

Between the transept and the apse there is a fairly deep space typical of some French models, in which the groundplan of Burgos cathedral is inspired. We shall remember that this space was originally taken up by the canons' choir, until this was moved to behind the transept in the 16th Century. This part of the apse, separated, as we shall see later, from the ambulatory by six screens designed in 1678 by Bernabé de Hazas and wrought by Juan de Arrillaga and Domingo de Guerzo, is now used for normal Cathedral services.

The floor of the chancel is raised, thus allowing for enhanced visibility. As early as the 16th Century it underwent alterations and was made of marble, jasper and slate. The modern floor is a 19th Century remodelling, the nine-step Carrara marble stairway up to it being finished in 1864.

Although they cannot always be seen, it is interesting to note that in the left-hand side of the presbytery there are several princes' tombs, built into the wall and partially hidden. This is historically important, as it carries ideological connotations, the princes being medieval. The tombs are those of Prince John (d. 1319), sixth son of Alfonso X and prince Sancho (d. 1374), Henry II's brother, together with a tombstone of the latter prince's wife, Princess Beatriz (d. 1381), daughter of King Peter of Portugal.

The end of the presbytery is dominated by the main reredos, dedicated to St Mary. The craftsmen involved in its making were mainly the sculptor Rodrigo de la Haya, with the collaboration of his brother Martín de la Haya, together with Simón de Berrieza and Domingo de Bérriz. In 1561, the work of some reliefs and an image for this altarpiece were already being paid for, the work being finished in 1580, to be gilded and polychromed from 1593 to 1596 by the painters Diego de Urbina and Gregorio Martínez. As well as these artists, mention must also be made of the sculptor Juan de Anchieta, paid in 1578 and 1583 for his groups of the Assumption and the Coronation, set in the upper part of the reredos.

The reredos is arranged in three tiers, plus a fourth smaller one, culminating in Calvary and divided vertically into a number of panels and interpanel spaces with reliefs and sculptures. The central panel houses the tabernacle, the image of St Mary the Great, the Assumption and Coronation of the Virgin by the Trinity. In the intercolumns of the three panels are the apostles, while the great reliefs show the following Marian themes (from bottom to top): Presentation and Purification; Birth of the Virgin and Visitation; Embrace before the Golden Gate and Annunciation and, in the final story, one of St Anne and a curious one of the Virgin and St Elizabeth and their children, the Boy Jesus and the little St John. Furthermore, among the reliefs of the last story we see St John the Baptist and the apostle St Matthew, while the lateral parts show St Luke and St Mark, the missing apostle St John apparently replaced by St John the Baptist, as the apostle is already represented in the intercolumns. The Calvary group crowns the reredos, but there are also statues of two angels at the sides: St Michael running the dragon through and the Guardian Angel, interestingly the guardian angel of the City of Burgos, a model of which he is holding.

Apart from the imagery and its expression, this reredos should be valued from other points of view. One is its architectural arrangement, related to that of the reredos of Astorga cathedral, as the structural rigour and the clarity of its parts herald the winds of change of the Counter-Reformation. Nevertheless, De la Haya's sculptures, though monumental, lack the compositional freedom and dynamic force of Anchieta's, more agile and Romanist in the Assumption and Coronation.

Right: The Reredos of the High Altar

Begun in 1561 by Rodrigo and Martín de la Haya and worked on by other artists (such as Juan de Anchieta, who did the Assumption and the Coronation), it was polychromed in the years 1593-96 by Diego de Urbina and Gregorio Martínez. It is a representation of the Apostles and Marian themes, the piece being dedicated to St Mary the Great, whose Gothic silver image presides it. Some aspects of the iconography are interesting, as is the importance given to the tabernacle, behoving to the ideals of Trent, and to the relics, for on the predella are St Victoria, St Centola and St Elena, saints particularly revered in the diocese.

Bottom: Footpace of the Reredos of the High Altar.

The footpace has an important ideological value owing to the reliquaries placed there with remains of St Centola, St Elena and St Victoria, whose martyrdoms are depicted in relief.

"St Tecla at the stake"
on the altarpiece of her chapel

An interesting Baroque sculpture thought
to be by Alejandro Carnicero. Though she
was a saint of the Roman period, the
iconographic detail of being martyred by
Moors is introduced. The chapel was built
with funding by Archbishop Manuel de
Samaniego y Jaca, from Tarragona,
where St Tecla is especially revered.

Other details on the retable concern the exaltation of the Eucharist and the relics, both of which are identified with the decisions of the Council of Trent. The first is represented in the manufacture in 1585 of a fine tabernacle, the work of Domingo de Bérriz, who conceived it as a large structure of three tiers with an upper finishing touch, covered in Eucharistic imagery. The work responds to the indications of 1575 contained in the Synodal Constitutions of the Burgos prelate Cardinal Francisco Pacheco, who required for the churches of his diocese "tabernacles of the worthiest and richest that it was possible to make". And as for the Trentine decree *de reliquiis sanctorum*, which sets store on the cult of relics, we can see that the retable of the main altar at Burgos bears reliefs and reliquaries concerning female saints venerated in the diocese: St Victoria and Saints Centola and Elena, whose relics were brought to Burgos in 1320 from Cologne and Siero, respectively.

Finally, in the centre of the altarpiece there is an outstanding image of the patron of the city and of the church, St Mary the Great, a beautiful Hispano-Flemish statue made in 1464, adorned with silver overlays. Seated, with the Child on her left knee, this fine sculpture was ordered by Bishop Luis de Acuña y Osorio, who in 1460 announced his wish to replace the old and small image with the one we can now contemplate, for which he donated the necessary silver and the Chapter gave 10,000 maravedíes. It was no surprise that the work should be entrusted to the goldsmith Cristóbal of Valladolid, who was then known as the "servant and silversmith to the Bishop". The silversmith Ferdinand of Oviedo is on record as having been entrusted with the making of a crown for the Virgin in 1488.

Left: *Dome of St Tecla's Chapel*

Top: *Pendentive of the dome of St Tecla's Chapel, with St Mark the Apostle.*

Four small Gothic chapels of the northern aisle were transformed into one large chapel on the initiative of Archbishop Manuel de Samaniego y Jaca, and built in 1731-35 from plans by Andrés Collado and Francisco Basteguieta, the centre being covered by a wonderful dome with polychromed plasterwork by Juan de Areche, and the evangelists on the pendentives.

The Northern Aisle of the Nave

The northern part of the church is next to the higher part of the city, so in medieval times there would have been little space for the building of chapels, those built lacking depth, a space being left behind with the parish chapel of St James of the Fountain (Santiago de la Fuente) and a piece of waste ground which was not really fitting. This situation started to improve at the end of the 15th Century with the building of a new chapel dedicated to St Anne and continued later with the Baroque Chapel of St Tecla.

ST TECLA'S CHAPEL

A walk round the chapels of this side begins at St Tecla's chapel. Its ground-plan includes the length of four original Gothic chapels (those of St Práxedes, St Victoria, All Saints and St Lucia), which, at the behest of Archbishop Manuel de Samaniego y Jaca, it replaced. It was dedicated to St Tecla, as she was much reve-red in the diocese of Tarragona, whence the prelate had come. The construction lasted from 1731 to 1735 and followed a plan by Andrés Collado (a resident of Lienda and master of works on the Royal Palace at Valsaín) and Francisco Basteguieta. It is a fine Baroque ensemble with vaults enlivened with plasterwork by Juan de Areche. In 1735, Narciso Cortés was paid for the cleaning of the cha-pel and the altarpiece, which means that the building was complete, the consecra-tion ceremonies of 1736 being of great importance. Some faults in the construc-tion must have been noticed, for Areche had to mend the plasterwork in 1740, and repairs to the stonework were carried out by Domingo de Ondátegui, Juan de

Following page: *Main altarpiece of St Tecla's Chapel.*

Thought to have been planned by Collado and Basteguieta, and because of its link with the local church of St Lawrence, it would not be surprising for it to have been executed by José Valdán, Bernardo López de Frías II and Manuel Romero Puelles, who worked there. The top shows Santiago Matamoros* with, at the sides, St Dominic de la Calzada and St Antón, who were associated with the Road to Santiago, which passed next to the chapel. (*=St James the Slayer of Moors, legend having it that St James's miraculous intervention at the Battle of Clavijo in the 9th Century was decisive in the Reconquest, translator's note.)

Sagarvinaga and Francisco Bazteguieta. These three men also built a small house over the sacristy and adjoining room, in the rear part of the chapel. Among the works of art inside the chapel, the most noteworthy is the ornate main altarpiece, built by the same masters as are thought to have designed the chapel, Collado and Basteguieta. It has gigantic downward-tapering columns bearing lively sculptures. The main niche contains St Tecla's martyrdom at the stake, attributed to Alejandro Carnicero, the sculptor from Iscar, whose studio was established in Salamanca at the time. It is curious to note that the fire is being anachronically kindled by two Moors, the saint having lived in Roman times. This group is flanked by sculptures of St Anthony the Abbot and St Dominic de la Calzada and above it there is a tabernacle with three small images of the Boy Christ the Saviour, St Ignatius and St Francis Xavier. The altarpiece is finished off in a semicircle with St James Matamoros (the Slayer of Moors) at the centre in a niche borne by two pairs of downward tapering pedestals and bearded terms. Two clypea with the images of St Joseph and St John the Baptist complete this attic, which has the armorial bearings of the Cathedral and of Archbishop Samaniego at its ends.

The left-hand side of the chapel, and the wall arches, are decorated with several Baroque reredoses, of the same style and period as the main one, dedicated respectively to the Trinity with All Saints, Our Lady of Grace, St Lucia and St Práxedes. Of outstanding historical interest is the 13th Century baptismal font, in the shape of a glass decorated with arches sheltering the apostles, the piece reminding us of the erstwhile parish character of St James of the Fountain, originally situated here. There are also some canvasses, including two painted in Rome at the beginning of the 18th Century depicting St John the Apostle and the Birth of the Baptist. Also noteworthy are a picture of iconographic interest of St Julian and some pieces of Baroque furniture.

The evangelists St Matthew and St John, on the main altarpiece of St Anne's Chapel.

CHAPEL OF THE CONCEPTION, OR ST ANNE'S CHAPEL

The next one is the Chapel of the Conception, or St Anne's Chapel, which takes up the space occupied previously by two small chapels dedicated to St Anne and St Antolín, and their back yard, so this chapel is quite large. For this purpose, in 1477, a representative of Bishop Luis de Acuña y Osorio asked permission to "build a chapel for our sepulchre... behind the chapels of St Anne and St Antolín... and it will be an elegant work and an adornment of the church." The two chapels in question were small and the outside was in a disreputable state, for, as Cathedral records say: "... what was there was so neglected and indecent that hardly anybody went there and so people committed improper acts and disservices to God there..."

Bishop Acuña's new chapel was built between 1477 and 1483 by John of Cologne and his son Simon, who finished it. Pieces from the original period include the Gothic screens at the entrance, made in 1495 by the screen-maker Luis de Paredes and, according to the records, "another tradesman from Palencia". Its cresting is decorated with griffins, castles, ogees and the prelate's arms.

There are several important works inside this chapel. The main altarpiece belongs to the period 1486-92 and to the gouge of the sculptor Gil de Siloe, who usually had the collaboration of the painter Diego de la Cruz (some details are by the painter Lanzuela, brought in at the behest of the Duke of Abrantes in 1868-70). The arrangement of the ensemble is a fusion of a tapestry with a conventional Gothic reredos. The retable depicts the Resurrection of Christ, accompanied by St Peter and St Paul, with the four evangelists at the sides and shields of Bishop Acuña on the piers. Above this, the ensemble is bordered by side panels with Gothic canopies over several scenes: Don Luis de Acuña with relatives and the appearance of Christ Crucified to St Eustaquio (or St Hipólito), the Birth and the

*Don Luis de Acuña's tomb
in St Anne's Chapel*

*Into the late Gothic atmosphere created by
Simon of Cologne and Gil de Siloe,
Renaissance taste is introduced with this
Archbishop's tomb, commissioned in 1519
from Diego de Siloe, who follows the
Roman model of Pope Sixtus IV.*

*Preceding pages: Main altarpiece of St
Anne's Chapel and detail.*

*Made in 1486-92 by the sculptor Gil de
Siloe, with polychromy by Diego de la Cruz,
this late-Gothic piece is arranged as a
triptych designed to contain a tapestry. The
main theme is dedicated to the genealogy of
the Virgin, arising from the upper part of
the Tree of Jesse - who lies prostrate
beneath - the shoots bearing the kings of his
line. Mary is flanked by allegories of the
Old and New Testaments (the former
blindfolded and with her sceptre broken. In
the bottom left-hand corner is the kneeling
figure of the funder of the chapel, Bishop
Luis de Acuña y Osorio.*

Presentation of the Virgin, the marriage of the Virgin to St Joseph, and St Joachim with the angel.

The most intricate composition is in the central space of the altarpiece, where the Virgin's immaculate condition is blended with the reality of her lineage, for which the artist used the tree of Jesse, who appears at the bottom, asleep, with his family tree growing out of his bosom, its shoots bearing the Kings of Judah surrounding the scene of St Joachim and St Anne's Embrace, the whole crowned by the image of the Virgin and Child. To the sides of this there are two allegories taken to be the Synagogue and the Church or the Old and New Testaments, consisting of two women with certain differences of detail: one, blindfolded with a veil, is holding the Tablets of the Law and a broken sceptre in her hands, while the other, her eyes uncovered, is holding a chalice and a whole sceptre. The ensemble is finished off in the normal way with the Calvary scene, which is flanked by the arms of the prelate who funded the reredos.

On the left of the entrance, inside Bishop Acuña's chapel, lies the tomb of Archdeacon Fernando Díaz de Fuentepelayo, a trusted and "very old servant" of the prelate, as the inscription says. It is usually attributed to Gil de Siloe because of its architectural organization and sculptural expressiveness, which are typical of the taste of the period round 1492 when Fuentepelayo died. Here his reclining effigy is holding a book and is accompanied by a page. On the side of the base, there are reliefs representing the Nativity (it was sometimes thought to be a theme concerning St Antolín, to whom the previous chapel had been dedicated) and the Adoration of the Magi. The ensemble is completed with a group concerning the Annunciation, God the Father, and angels bearing Fuentepelayo's shield.

St Anne's Chapel having been built in times of artistic change, in the centre we find an extraordinary piece belonging to the Renaissance: the sepulchre itself of Luis de Acuña. Although the prelate had died in 1495, his sepulchral monument was not considered until the executor of his will signed a two-hundred-ducat contract with Diego de Siloe in 1519. Diego was the son of the Gothic craftsman Gil de Siloe, but had been trained in the Italy of the Renaissance, where he had flourished. So, here in Burgos, Diego follows the Italian model used in Rome by Pollaiolo for the sepulchre of Pope Sixtus IV. In Burgos, Siloe reiterates the originality of the relatively low base, which allows the reclining bishop resting on it to stand out more, while the sides are concave, and the corners are finished off with lion's paws ending in acanthus leaves and scrolls. A series of reliefs adorns the sides and ends of the base, with allegories of the Virtues and shields of the bishop. On the edge an inscription proclaims the honour of his line and the date of his death: *PROPTER VTRVMQVE LATVS PRAESVL LUDOVICUS ACUÑA OSSORIO STIRPES QVAS ADAMAVIT HABET. ANNO MCDXCV.* Attention should be given to the expressive quality of the piece, especially regarding the reclining body, which, as was then normal, appears to be intended as a likeness.

There is also a small stone altarpiece dedicated to St Anne Triple (with the Virgin and Child), together with images of St Bartholomew and St Vítores, commissioned from Diego de Siloe in 1522, though, in the opinion of Gómez Moreno, its quality betrays it as being more the work of de Siloe's studio than of the master himself.

There is an interesting painting of the Holy Child with the little St John, a Renaissance work of great correction attributed to the Italian painter Andrea del Sarto, as it bears a relationship with a similar work of his hanging in the Barberini Gallery in Rome.

The Northern Arm of the Transept

We have already mentioned how the lie of the land affected the building of the cathedral, and that the left-hand side of the church was to be lacking in space. For this reason, in the northern arm of the transept there is only one chapel, St Nicholas's, while at the end, access to the northern entrance is offered by the Golden Stairway.

THE GOLDEN STAIRWAY

The monumental Golden Stairway was build at the behest of Bishop Juan Rodríguez de Fonseca (1514-24). We shall remember that the Apostles' Door, or *Coronería* (Leatherworkers') Door situated in the northern part of the transept is on considerably higher ground than the rest of the Cathedral, the problem of the vertical difference being solved in the medieval period by another stairway, which, apart from being difficult to negotiate, was the subject of irreverent abuse by persons walking between the higher and lower parts of the city (in documents drawn up in 1465, the public are asked not to walk through with "wineskins or jars, meat or live animals, poultry, kids or lambs...". Bishop Fonseca had it taken down and a side door - the Skinners' Door - put in. This brought about unrest and protest, which caused the prelate to have a new stairway built to communicate with the Apostles' Door.

It was planned by the young Diego de Siloe in 1519, shortly after his return from Italy, and the main construction work was finished by 1522, when the Frenchman Master Hilario had begun to work on the wrought iron balustrades and handrails, this being finished with the work of the silversmiths Espinosa and Juan de Orna in 1526.

Diego de Siloe's ingenious solution to the constraints of the place, whereby a single straight initial flight divides into two, which, bending back from two half-landings come together again at the top, has long been the subject of much praise.

Preceding page: The Golden Stairway.

The problem of the difference in height between the Coronería *Door and the transept is overcome by this staircase, built in 1519-22 by the Renaissance artist Diego de Siloe, with banisters by the French master craftsman Hilario. The remarkable architectural solution is inspired by Bramante's project for the Cortile del Belvedere in Rome. The Grotesque reliefs, based on engravings, are also noteworthy.*

*The Southern Aisle,
seen from the Transept.*

It is somewhat similar to Michelangelo's design for the Laurentian Library in Florence. As Wethey demonstrated, the young Diego de Siloe must have found inspiration for the Golden Stairway in Bramante's project for the "Cortile del Belvedere", which he may have seen during his early stay in Rome. Apart from the architectural design, the motifs decorating the stairway are also to be taken into account. They are a great novelty as they suppose a recent Hispanic incorporation of grotesque models which at the time were known from engravings. Thus the fantastic animal ridden by a naked man carrying a card is based on Nicoletto Rosex da Modena; the floral chalices are inspired by Agostino de Musi, as are the winged beasts at the foot of the stairs and other animal designs; the grotesque figures of the intrados of the arch are derived from Giovanni da Brescia; the sphinx with the serpent's tail and the gallinaceous sphinx are copies of Agostino Veneziano. There is also an echo of Michelangelo in the use of scallop shells with the base upwards and in the human figures inspired by his famous "ignudi".

ST NICHOLAS'S CHAPEL

The only chapel opening off the northern arm of the transept is St Nicholas's, one of the oldest parts of the temple mentioned in documents, as work is on record as going on there in 1230, which is born out by the architecture. The artistic elements it contains are simple, as is the case of blurred reminder of the man who funded it, the choirmaster Pedro Díaz de Villahoz (d. 1230) or the tomb of a relative of his, Bishop Juan de Villahoz (1268-69), under an *arcosolium* on the left, his reclining effigy protected by a baskethandle arch resting on human heads. The late Gothic screen over the entrance is early 16th Century. The altarpiece, made in the second third of the 17th Century, is dedicated to Christ's Nativity, and has a St Nicholas at the top.

Opposite the chapel, on the west wall of the transept, there hangs a large painting of the "Miracle of St John de Ortega", a well-known Burgos saint connected with the Road to Santiago, the layout and wayside hostelries of which he favoured in the Montes of Oca to the east. This picture, donated to the Cathedral by Archbishop Navarrete in 1718, was painted by a disciple of Antonio Palomino, the Biscayan painter Nicolás Antonio de la Cuadra.

The Northern Side of the Ambulatory

In the thickened portion of wall between St Nicholas's Chapel and the beginning of the ambulatory, a spiral staircase ascends to the upper part of the church and the tambour. The wall next to the door leading to it is rendered aesthetically interesting by a beautiful sepulchre.

THE SEPULCHRE OF
DON PEDRO FERNANDEZ DE VILLEGAS

Indeed, at the beginning of the north side of the ambulatory is the tomb of Don Pedro Fernández de Villegas, Archdeacon of Burgos and member of the Cathedral Chapter, an educated man and a poet, an influential personage during the transition from the 15th Century to the 16th. In 1503 the archdeacon was given permission by the Chapter to use this singular location to arrange his interment, which, though not documented is thought to be the work of Simon of Cologne, as the prebendary was in this artist's debt in 1510, and the sepulchre is typical of the work of his studio. It is a late Gothic piece with an *arcosolium* in the wall, dense iconography and Gothic traceries, of a type oft-repeated in the Burgos area and in the circles of Siloe and the Cologne (it is very similar to Díez de Fuentepelayo's sepulchre). The main arch, of the basket-handle type, with openwork on its intrados, is surmounted by an ogee arch extradosed with *crockets*. It is flanked by Gothic pilasters with canopies and pedestals reaching up to enclose in the upper part an ensemble of geometric and figurative motifs. The deceased is represented reclining on a bed born by lions, the front of which is decorated with the arms of the departed supported by pages, while in the centre are St Peter and St Paul, under canopies. The wall under the arch shows the Purification of the Virgin, while above the arch is the deceased's shield, shown again on a higher pedestal where the seated figure of God the Father presides the scene of the Annunciation, with a vase of Madonna lilies. The side pilasters bear small sculptures on two levels: the lower ones are dedicated to St Andrew, St John the Evangelist, the Baptist and St James. The upper ones are of Fathers of the Church and Saints (Francis, Nicholas, George).

THE CHAPEL OF THE NATIVITY

The Chapel of the Nativity is the first one on this side of the ambulatory. It takes up what were originally two sections, where there used to be chapels dedicated to St Giles and St Martin, where in the 13th Century, Bishops Don Juan (d. 1246), Chancellor to King Ferdinand III, and Don Martín González de Contreras (d. 1267) were buried. In 1577, Doña Ana de Espinosa, widow of Pedro de González de Salamanca, announced the arrival in Spain of a large quantity of silver bars and coins amassed by her family in America and shipped from Peru to build a funerary chapel for her family in the Cathedral.

To this end, in 1560, an agreement was reached by Doña Ana de Espinosa and her daughters María and Catalina de Salamanca, on the one hand, and the Cathedral Chapter on the other, whereby they would be granted the Chapels of St Giles and St Martin in exchange for adequate monetary compensation. In 1562 work, under the supervision of the master stonemason Martín de Bérriz, was already in progress on the new chapel, which was dedicated to the Nativity. By about 1580, the work must have been practically complete, as other complementary work was going on. This includes the stained glasswork by Pedro de Arce and the two screens ordered from Leonys de León in 1583. The stonework begun by Martín de Bérriz was finished by Martín de la Haya. The architecture is Mannerist, the space being covered by an oval dome with polychrome painting by Juan de Cea. Around the central lantern giving zenithal light to the chapel there are reliefs of the Evangelists by Domingo de Bérriz, the Fathers of the Church being set out on the pendentives.

The altarpiece of this Chapel is outstanding, part of it is stonework, blending in with the very fabric of the building, and enclosing another, more conventional, wooden structure. The sculptors Martín de la Haya and Domingo de Bérriz are on record as having worked on it during the 1580s, while the polychromy is by Juan de Cea and Constantino of Naples. This is a Romanist Mannerist work of the type becoming popular at the time in Castile. The arrangement of supports of gigantic size at the sides or the use of columns with the lowest third carved and the rest fluted - sometimes in spirals - are typical of the Classicist structure of Romanism, of which another characteristic feature is the gesticulating style of the sculpture, with histrionic, idealized types, in which the influence of Anchieta, Guillén and other Romanists is already to be noticed. As for iconography, the intercolumns of the *arcosolium* in the wall contain St Peter, St Paul, St Anne and St Catherine, and

The Ambulatory.

The ambulatory was cut off from the Chancel by a set of reliefs. At the beginning of the Renaissance, Bigarny made the three in the centre. The closing off was to be completed in 1681-83 with one more scene at each side, like this "Prayer in the Garden". Shortly afterwards, the pillars were decorated with statues, echoing those on the right; these are the ones placed by Cologne to flank the access to the High Constable's Chapel, which is protected by a screen by Cristóbal de Andino.

there are reliefs of angels on the upper spandrels of the arch, the intrados of which is decorated with squares containing hanging fleurons. The arch encloses the altarpiece itself, where there are six great reliefs distributed in two tiers; the central panel contains the Nativity - the advowson of the chapel - with the Adoration of the Magi above it; the lower portions of the side panels show the Presentation of the Virgin and the Embrace at the Golden Gate, while their upper tiers depict the Visitation and the Annunciation; the altarpiece culminates in the habitual Calvary scene.

Attention should be given to the stalls, contemporary with the altarpiece and by the same sculptor, Martín de la Haya, who received nearly three hundred thousand maravedíes for them. They have a set of reliefs dedicated to the Annunciation, theological virtues and cardinal virtues. The stalls make it difficult to view today the Gothic tombs of the bishops buried in the original chapels in the 13th Century, Don Juan and Don Martín González de Contreras.

THE CHAPEL OF THE ANNUNCIATION

The next chapel is that of the Annunciation (formerly St Antón's Chapel), whose architecture is the original 13th Century Gothic from when the chapel was dedicated to St Anthony the Abbot, according to a letter of foundation of the chaplaincy of that advowson from the time of Bishop Gonzalo García de Gudiel (1276-80). At the beginning of 1540 this chapel was requested as a burial place by Canon Juan Martínez de San Quirce, who promised to refurbish it. To this end, on the 16th August 1540, Canon San Quirce engaged the sculptor Juan de Lizarazu to make an altarpiece in which the architectural elements would have to be "wrought in the Roman (style)" and "German blue" was to be used in the painting and hangings, and certain images were to be included. Consequently, the altarpiece is arranged with balusters and a set of niches for figures, the gilding and the head of the cherubim on the blue background being especially worthy of note. The footpace, which is quite large, centres on a delicately worked Annunciation, flanked by St John the Baptist (patron saint of Canon San Quirce) and St Antón (after whom the Chapel is named). The main tier shows the wounds of Ecce Homo, accompanied by St Sebastian and St Roque, both also wounded; the second tier shows St Jerome, flanked by St John the Evangelist (another patron saint of Canon San Quirce) and St Catherine (patron saint of theologians and the good death). At the top there is a shield with the wounds of Christ, supported by angels, culminating in the bust of God the Father.

We suppose that in the 16th Century, when work was done on the altarpiece, sepulchres, etc., the archway leading to the chapel was altered, the old Gothic pointed arch being replaced with a round one with a set of rosettes on the intrados, an innovation which also affected the adjoining Chapel of St Gregory.

The name St Anthony the Abbot was changed in 1636, when this chapel was granted, to Don Juan de Torre Ayala, then Bishop of Ciudad Rodrigo and formerly Canon and Cathedral schoolmaster at Burgos, who decided on the new advowson of the Chapel of the Annunciation.

ST GREGORY'S CHAPEL

Here too the original 13th Century Gothic architectural structure is maintained, the only alteration having been the archway at the entrance, carried out in the 16th Century, when a round arch intradosed with rosettes was built, the entrance being protected by a contemporary Renaissance screen. There is a remarkable painting of the "Martyrdom of St Peter", inspired by an original by Guido Reni, and which is identified with the work concerning the same theme painted in 1646 by Mateo Cerezo (the father). There is also an interesting 18th Century sculpture of St Bruno brought from the demolished Convent of Victory (the courthouse was built on its site in the 19th Century). The image of St Gregory is 18th Century, perhaps the one made by Manuel Romero Ortiz for an old altarpiece of 1774, which had polychromy and gilding carried out by the painter Camino in 1776.

From the artistic and historical points of view, the most important things in St Gregory's Chapel are the Gothic tombs of two Burgos prelates of the 14th Century: Don Gonzalo de Hinojosa (d. 1327) and Don Lope de Fontecha (d. 1351), the latter being richer, with an *arcosolium*. What matters in both cases is the iconography, as the typology of the reclining figure is similar, while the motifs on the fronts of the bases are prime examples of disciplinary rules or changes in habits and tastes. Indeed, it was a medieval custom to establish an atmosphere of mourning and sensitivity during funerals, which even penetrated the religious ceremonies, with gesticulating laments, wailers, etc. The commotions occasioned inside the Cathedral led the chapter of Burgos cathedral in 1334 to forbid "rela-

tives, friends or other men to go to the choir stalls or weep in the choir area during mass and while the body was in the choir area except at the entrance when bringing the body in or removing it to the grave for burial".

The two interments mentioned in this Chapel, one before and one after the year 1334, reflect an iconographic change which seems to be based on this prohibition. Thus, on the older tomb, that of Don Gonzalo de Hinojosa (d. 1327), there are anecdotal scenes from a funeral procession with figures wailing and gesticulating at the enshrouding of the corpse. This subject is missing from the later sepulchre of Don Lope de Fontecha (1351), which is more monumental, showing an aesthetic change, as well as an iconographic one. Beside the reclining effigy, thurifying angels evoke the funeral antiphony "In Paradisum", in which angels are said to descend from Heaven and to cense the deceased, who is accompanied by the prayers of an ecclesiastical procession.

There is also, inside the *arcosolium*, a pediment with the scene of the "Deesis", in which intercession is made before Christ the Judge for the soul of the dead man, evoking the model over the *Coronería* Door of the previous century; this subject is associated with the angels holding the instruments of the passion on the intrados of the arch: the spear, cross, crown, hammer, sponge, column and whip. On the front of the base, Gothic canopies overhang scenes of the Adoration of the Magi: on the right, the Nativity, in the middle, the crowned Virgin with the Child on her lap, with St Joseph and a Wise Man in the background, while on the left, the other two Magi approach the Child, accompanied by the prophet Isaiah, or by David. Over this sepulchre there is a raised gable adorned by statuettes of the twelve apostles with the figure of Christ as the finishing touch. The gable contains the Coronation of the Virgin by Jesus, accompanied by angels with candles and a censer.

Reliefs and Sculptures
of the Retrochoir and Ambulatory

The pillars and intercolumns surrounding the deep chancel have lost their original Gothic appearance as time has caused changing tastes and the accumulation of images to concentrate on this privileged part of the ambulatory. So the five central intercolumns, those of the retrochoir, were filled with great stone reliefs and the six remaining arches had their pillars adorned with a set of sculptures protected by screens. The three central arches of the ambulatory were finished at the end of the 15th Century and beginning of the 16th, while two others, one on each side of the first three, were made in the 18th Century, when the rest of the ambulatory was decorated.

It is known that in mid 1497, "the retrochoir of the church was begun" and then Simon of Cologne began his collaboration in the work, being in charge of directing the works and making the ornaments for the pillars, tabernacles, canopies, figures, etc., used to frame three great compositions in the retrochoir. The three reliefs, however, were made by the Burgundian Philippe de Bigarny, who was to remain linked with the city of Burgos after this his first commission there. On the 17th July, 1498 he was asked to prepare the "Way to Calvary", which he finished in March of the following year, together with the apostles arranged on the lower tier, and doubtlessly owing to the success of his work, on the 18th March 1499, he was asked to make two other large reliefs dedicated to the "Crucifixion" and the "Descent and Resurrection", together with eight images for its predella, the first one being put in place in 1500 and the last in 1503. Bigarny's work caused a great impression in Gothicist Burgos, the artist incorporating

Top: *View of the Retrochoir.*
In 1498 the Burgundian Philippe de Bigarny was commissioned to execute a relief to close off the retrochoir, two others being made in 1500 and 1503. These three reliefs constitute a first fruit of the Renaissance, in a late Gothic environment.

Top left: *Detail of the tomb of Bishop Gonzalo de Hinojosa, in St Gregory's Chapel. This personage (d. 1327) was notable for building St Catherine's Chapel in the cloister and for bringing the relics of St Centola and St Elena from Siero, on the banks of the Ebro, and those of St Victoria from Cologne. On his sepulchre, the mourning scene shows him being enshrouded before a cortège of gesticulating people who are weeping and pulling their hair out.*

Bottom left: *St Ferdinand, in the ambulatory.*

63

Renaissance realism into the great figures of the foreground, although in the compositions and backgrounds, a certain medieval heaviness is evident. We shall take the liberty of drawing attention to a clearly humanistic iconographic detail included in his first relief: the "Way to Calvary", where the jambs of the city gate are adorned with a decoration of candelabra, with Cupid-like figures on the frieze, the capitals being especially interesting, with representations of Hercules, referring to the mythological idea Hercules = Christ.

To these three reliefs of the centre of the retrochoir, a further two were added in the 17th Century as part of the improvements promoted by Archbishop Enrique Peralta y Cárdenas (1665-79), who requited the Chapter's generosity in granting him a large space for his funerary chapel by funding the complete closing-in of the deep chancel. In 1677 he commissioned Master Bernardo de Hazas to draw up a plan, which fitted in with the Chapter's criterion of continuing with previous styles (eschewing a Classicist arrangement of the architecture, as might appear fitting for the period). So a further panel on each side of the retrochoir was closed

Aspects of the Retrochoir.

Philippe de Bigarny sculpted some reliefs with Renaissance novelties in their forms and expressive devices, although the Gothic tradition still appears in the compositions. One's attention is drawn, in the relief of the Road to Calvary, to the fact that the city gate bears reliefs of Hercules, a mythological motif allegorizing Christ.

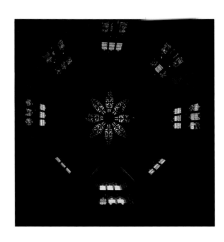

*The High Constable's Chapel.
It was built from 1482 by Simon of
Cologne for the High Constable of Castile
Don Pedro Fernández de Velasco and his
wife Doña Mencía de Mendoza. Its
greatness is announced by its size,
heraldry and tombs.*

with a relief on each one, the remaining pillars in the ambulatory were adorned and their arches were protected with screens. In 1678 the stonework was commissioned from Bernabé Hazas and Francisco de Pontón, the sculpture being put in the hands of the prolific northerner Fernando de la Peña. The two large reliefs, however, were effected in 1681-83 by Pedro Alonso de los Ríos from Valladolid, who enjoyed great prestige in court in Madrid at the time. These reliefs are of the "Prayers in the Garden" and the "Ascension", where Alonso de los Ríos displays correctness and the oneness of composition typical of the Baroqueness of his style.

The ribs built onto the piers of the ambulatory are decorated with motifs of ribbons and vegetables and a set of pedestals and canopies to house numerous saints revered in the church at the time, some of them, like St Vítores, St Centola, St Elena, St Victoria, etc., having especial significance for Burgos. Then, the six remaining arches that are not filled in are protected with screens designed by Bernabé de Hazas in 1678 and commissioned from Juan de Arrillaga and Domingo de Guerzo. The death of the prelate Peralta (although he had the support of his successor Archbishop Isla) caused some delays to the work on this part of the ambulatory, culminated in 1704-06 with the finishing of its sculptures by Francisco González de Sisniega and the gilding of the screens by Lucas de la Concha.

The Chapel of the Purification, or High Constable's Chapel

The most sumptuous part of the Cathedral is the Chapel of the Purification, off the centre of the ambulatory, better known as the "High Constable's Chapel", as it was built for the High Constable of Castile at the end of the 15th Century. The original Gothic chapel had been dedicated to St Peter, and among the medieval bishops buried in it were Rodríguez Quexada and Domingo Arroyuelo. After 1374 it also became known as Count Sancho's Chapel, after the memorial service held here on the death of that prince, brother of Henry II (his tomb is in the chancel).

One of the most highly regarded families at the time of the Catholic Monarchs was that formed by the marriage of the High Constable of Castile, Don Pedro Fernández de Velasco and Doña Mencía de Mendoza, as it brought together outstanding lines. Doña Mencía is said to have promised her husband a palace to live in, land for recreation and a chapel as his last resting place. Of these promises, the High Constable was only to reap the benefits of the third, for he died on the 6th January 1492, though the High Constable's Chapel and his palace, known as the Casa del Cordón ("House of the Ribbon") still exist today.

Doña Mencía came from a family of artistic sensitivity and with literary tastes cultivated in post-humanism (she was the daughter of the Marquis of Santillana and sister of Cardinal Pedro González de Mendoza, considered to be "the third King of Spain"), so her tendency to patronize works of art should come as no surprise, and it was she who took direct charge of the building of the chapel. On the 1st July 1482, the Cathedral Chapter granted Countess Mencía the space of St Peter's Chapel for her to build the resting place that she intended.

The building was put in the hands of the most prestigious architect of the moment, Simon of Cologne, who topped out the chapel in 1494 with a wonderful openwork vault, although certain minor works of sculpture and furniture were yet to be carried out. As the High Constable died in 1492, before his chapel was finished, the Chapter authorized his provisional burial in the chancel, where he lay for three years. The basic part of the construction may be considered as having been finished in 1517, with the building of the sacristy by Francisco de Colonia, son of the master craftsman who built the chapel.

The building has is centrally planned, as is normal for funerary chapels and, although there are antecedents, this work was to be a point of reference for many others inspired by it for other Spanish churches. Its volume is arranged on a polygonal groundplan, somewhat irregular because of the architectural circumstances of the Cathedral. The elevation has a solid lower part lightened in appearance by the great shields of the founders, the Fernández de Velasco and the Mendoza-Figueroa. Above this a storey is hollowed out with a narrow triforium of wide engrailed arches, with savages supporting other family arms. The walls are finished with a double crown of high stained-glass windows that lighten the stellate vault covering the whole, which includes a central star of inter-rib tracery, with a boss representing the Purification of the Virgin, the advowson of the chapel.

Vault of the High Constable's Chapel

The airiness, beauty and openness were echoed by other chapels with windows and openwork vaults built in the 16th Century.

*Door of the sacristy in the
High Constable's Chapel*

*When the building was completed during
the height of the Renaissance, the door
was decorated with Plateresque designs.
The tympanum shows the Holy Cross, to
which the Mendoza were linked.*

Right: *Tomb of the High Constable and
his wife.*

*On a reddish jasper base lie the reclining
effigies of Don Pedro Fernández de
Velasco and Doña Mencía de Mendoza.
Uncertainty exists as to the identity of the
sculptor, who may have been Alonso
Berruguete, Juan de Lugano or Philippe
de Bigarny, the last mentioned being
considered the most probable today. Soft
forms, correctness of execution, and a
master craftsman's thoroughness
dominate the piece.*

Apart from the impressive architecture, due value must also be given to the wealth of sculpture and other artistic elements contained in this chapel. Such artistic and iconographic profusion is to be noted as soon as one reaches the entrance door, where there is a decoration of religious scenes (Nativity, Purification and Annunciation), emblems (a unicorn, lions, a cross potenty and the monogram IHS) and shields repeated in several works funded by the High Constables.

The screen protecting the entrance is also valuable, being a noteworthy Renaissance piece wrought by the screen-maker Cristóbal Andino in 1523, with the date and the artist's name engraved on the inside (AB ANDINO/A.D.MDXXIII).

The chapel is designed for funerary purposes and so the central tomb of the High Constable and his wife, and the altar stand out.

In the centre lies the double sepulchre of the High Constable Don Pedro Fernández de Velasco and his wife Doña Mencía de Mendoza. There is much discrepancy as to who made this double tomb for the first High Constable and his wife, the sculptors Bigarny, Alonso Berruguete and John of Lugano vying for this consideration. The reclining couple are attired as befits their worthy social condition and are represented with a certain softness of form, thoroughness in the anatomic intentions of the likenesses, in the quality of the cloths, armour and other details of dress. It is most likely that the work was carried out by the city's most accomplished sculptor of the period, Philippe de Bigarny. Between 1525 and 1532, this artist received several sums for making the base of the sepulchre and for sculpting the reclining forms from the marble which he had had imported from Genoa for the purpose.

Next to this piece there is a large block of reddish jasper ordered in 1552 for the tomb of the fourth High Constable (grandson and namesake of the chapel's founder, whence the uncertainties concerning the sepulchre) and his wife Juliana Angela de Aragón, which was never made as the commission was granted to Alonso Berruguete, when he was already working on important projects in Toledo, and who subsequently died.

The work on the main altar of the chapel presiding over the head of the tomb was carried out over the period 1523-26 by the sculptors Philippe de Bigarny and Diego de Siloe, with gilding and polychromy by the painter León Picardo. The architectural structure of the piece is novel, as a large space is given over to the principal group, in the form of a stage showing the Purification. The sculptures reveal the different approaches of the sculptors to their work: the thoroughness of Bigarny with the Priest and the Prophetess Anne, and the classicism of Siloe in the group on the left comprising the Virgin and St Joseph with the Child together with a companion. They also shared the work on the predella and the second story, with three representations of Christ (praying in the transfiguration, tied to the column and with the cross) and in the Calvary scene at the top. Furthermore, on the columns flanking the ensemble are the allegories of the Church (by Siloe) and the Synagogue (by Bigarny).

Various works contributed to enrich this chapel, many of which have been preserved, such as the side altarpieces, which reveal the change in taste that took place after the beginning, from Gothic to Renaissance. On the right there is the small altarpiece of St Anne, of Gothic architecture, and late Hispano-Flemish figures attributed to the sculptor Gil de Siloe, though some of the Renaissance pieces will be by his son Diego (St Marina, Mary Magdalen and Christ's Body born by angels). The other side altarpiece, on the left, is the Renaissance altarpiece of St Peter, finished in 1523, and on which Philippe de Bigarny and Diego de Siloe worked together, the polychromy being by León Picardo, who was paid for his work during the period 1523-32. Among the statuary, one's attention is usually caught by the little side image of St Jerome, which bears the typical signs of

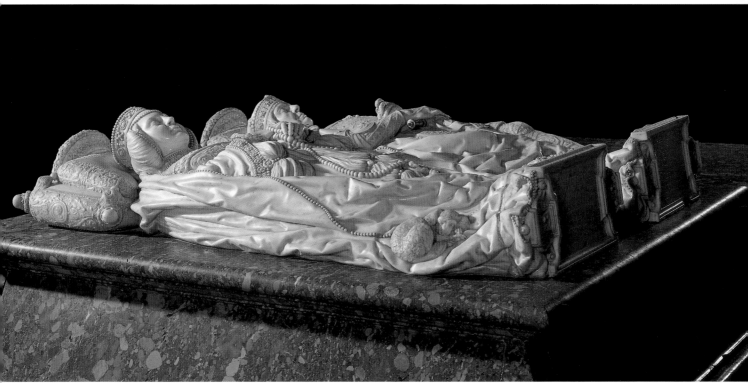

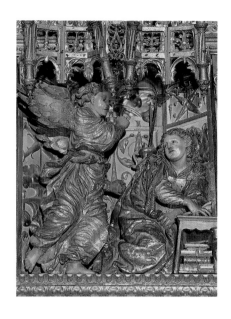

Main altarpiece of the High Constable's
Chapel.

Between 1523 and 1526, Diego de Siloe
and Philippe de Bigarny worked together
on this beautiful reredos which opens up
like a stage to show the group of the
Purification, where the two masters' styles
are contrasted: the Holy Family, on the
left, is more classical, whereas the priest
and the prophetess Anne on the right are
more thorough. Higher up, on the sides,
are the allegories of the Old and New
Testaments (or the Synagogue and the
Church).
Philippe de Bigarnys's Annunciation
likewise contrasts with the gougework of
Diego de Siloe on the Visitation and
Nativity.

Top: *Triptych of the Virgin and Child, in the High Constable's Chapel.*

This was painted around 1530 in Brussels by the "Master of the Legend of Mary Magdalen", who may be identified as Bernaert van der Stock. It was bequeathed to this chapel in 1846 by a churchman.

Right: *"Mary Magdalen" in the High Constable's Chapel.*

The fourth High Constable, grandson and namesake of the founder, Duke of Frías and Count of Haro, gave this impressive painting of Mary Magdalen to the chapel. Its "sfumatto", reminiscent of Leonardo, allows us to attribute it to Gian Pietro Ricci. It is mentioned in the 1548 inventory and now hangs in the sacristy.

Siloe's gouge. The scant Renaissance seating of eleven stalls by Philippe de Bigarny was finished in 1528.

There are several artistic pieces of remarkable value, only some of which we shall mention. One is the Triptych of the Virgin and Child, hitherto attributed to Gerard David. Elisa Bermejo thinks that it was made in Brussels around 1530 by the so-called "Master of the Legend of Mary Magdalen", who may be identified as Bernaert van der Stock, with the influence of Van der Weyden and Van Orley. The central panel shows a country scene, with the Virgin sitting in a meadow on red cushions, with the Child on her lap eating from a bunch of grapes offered by an angel, clearly an allegory of the Eucharist and Redemption. The left-hand panel shows a simple Nativity group above which, as though set on an upper floor, is a small Annunciation scene set in a Gothic interior. The right-hand panel is dedicated to the Presentation, again with Gothic motifs in grisaille on the altar table and on the reredos showing Moses.

There are also pictures of the founders or of religious subjects, including an important canvass of Christ Crucified, called "Christ of Agony", a realist work of great quality painted by the Burgos painter Mateo Cerezo around 1662-63.

In the sacristy, some of the former splendour remains, such as several pieces of silver, jet and ivory, and a Mary Magdalen by the painter Gian Pietro Ricci, a disciple of Leonardo. Outstanding among the silverwork is the censer with a representation of the temptation of Adam and Eve, where the serpent is shown with a woman's head.

Before leaving the High Constable's Chapel, one should notice the presence next to the entrance of two tombs of prelates of Burgos of the 14th Century, where we may appreciate the iconographic change indicated by the examples in St Gregory's Chapel concerning the gesticulations of mourning which were prohibited in the Cathedral by the Chapter in 1334. Such scenes are thus represented on Bishop Pedro Rodríguez Quexada's sepulchre (d. 1313), but are absent from that of Domingo de Arroyuelo (d. 1380).

ESTAIMAGEN·DIO·AESTA·SVCAPILLA DON·PERO ERNANDEZ·DE VELASCO·QVARTO CONDESTABLE·DE·LOS·DE TILLA·DE LOS DE SVLIN AGE·DVQE DE FRIAS·ECON DE·DE ARO ECETER

The Southern Side of the Ambulatory

ST JAMES'S CHAPEL

St James's Chapel has an irregular groundplan, as the original one was altered in the 16th Century after the building of the adjoining High Constable's Chapel to make use of the space between that chapel and the cloister. It also opened out into the neighbouring St John's Chapel, although today they are separated by a low wall (St John's Chapel thus becomes the Museum, entered from the cloister). The new construction of St James's Chapel is by the architect Juan de Vallejo, who worked on it from 1521 to 1534, finding difficulties in making the wide vault with its complex pattern of tracery and curved ribs, in the style that was then spreading from Burgos. The back wall has an arch with an engrailed intrados with figures of the Annunciation, Adam and Eve and St James, thought to be of the school of Diego de Siloe.

We shall begin our appreciation of the works of art in this chapel with the screen over the entrance, made by Bartolomé Elorza of Elgóibar in 1696.

Replacing older ones, the present main altarpiece was designed in 1772 by the architect Fernando González de Lara, who followed the Classicist tastes in vogue at the time, although some echoes of decoration are retained: sculptures are included of St James, the Immaculate, St John the Evangelist and María Salomé. Among other works is a picture of St Francis painted by Mateo Cerezo shortly after the middle of the 17th Century.

This place was selected for several burials as long ago as the medieval period (for example, that of Bishop Villacreces, in 1404). After the substantial alterations of the 16th Century, some new Renaissance sepulchres were made. Next to the entrance, on the left, there is the sepulchre of Don Juan Ortega de Velasco, the Abbot of St Quirce, commissioned from Juan de Vallejo, who introduced artistic novelties in the placing of the reclining body on the original sarcophagus as well as in the "boundary markers" flanking the ensemble. The tympanum shows the Baptism of Christ, the Immaculate disposed in the upper part with tondi of St Peter and St Paul, culminating in a bust of God the Father crowned by the Calvary group. The prebendary arms figure on shields supported by little angels repeated on the acroteria and foot-pace.

Another interesting sepulchre is that of Lesmes de Astudillo and his wife Mencía de Paredes, made in 1542. It is of the *arcosolium* type with the reclining effigies made of slate - typical of Burgos - and with the Adoration of the Magi on the tympanum. Above this is the relief of the Purification, and the whole is finished off with Christ resuscitated over a pediment containing the Virgin and Child. Next to this sepulchre there is an *arcosolium* similar in style to the former, but with different structural and ornamental details. It may have housed another sepulchre, perhaps of members of the Astudillos-Paredes family, buried in the neighbouring plot, for the shields would seem to indicate thus. The altar is dedicated to the Annunciation, a subject repeated in the painting set in the back and in the relief of the second story of the monument, where it is flanked by statues of St John the Baptist and St John the Evangelist, the whole finished off with God the Father on the tympanum, over which there is a Crucifixion. The picture of the Annunciation is by the Valladolid painter Gregorio Martínez, whose collaboration was sought because towards the end of the 16th Century he was working on the polychromy of the High Altar of the cathedral.

Cathedral Sacristy

The furniture is also the work of Friar José San Juan de la Cruz, and is Rococo, as are the images of St Julian and St Indalecio, saints venerated in the diocese. Its apsidal end is covered with plasterwork, where the Baroqueness culminates in a Coronation of the Virgin by the Trinity, with a great retinue of angels and musicians.

THE SACRISTY

Another room off the ambulatory is the Sacristy, which has always been here, lit by windows onto the ambulatory and onto the cloisters, and with doors to both places. Making use of Archbishop Juan Francisco Guillén's legacy of eight thousand ducats, in 1761 the Chapter agreed to renew the structure of the sacristy, engaging for the purpose Friar José de San Juan de la Cruz, a barefoot Carmelite from the Monastery at Logroño. Together with its anteroom, it has a rectangular groundplan with an apse, its walls consisting of panels strengthened by piers with compound capitals, the whole being covered by an elliptical vault on pendentives, with a lantern. In the vaulting and other high parts, there is a great density of plasterwork, especially on the main wall, with the Coronation of the Virgin or the later Annunciation, where a small plaque says "Anno Domini 1765".

The furniture is of the same period, Friar José de San Juan de la Cruz also having looked after the design of the drawers, for which he bore in mind those of the Salesian Monastery in Madrid, the result being a piece with decorative details of Rococo taste. The same style is used for the three altars of the apse furnished with "tables with areas of lapis lazuli with veins of gold to be smooth and shiny", as the records state, and adorned with mirrors. The furnishings are illustrated by a set of pictures of the life of Jesus from the studio of Luca Giordano. There are also two statues between the altarpieces of St Julian and St Indalecio, singularly revered in Burgos, which reflect Rococo animation.

ST HENRY'S CHAPEL

The last two sections of the ambulatory belong to St Henry's Chapel, which may also be entered from the transept. It is a chapel formed in the second half of the 17th Century by uniting the space of two older ones. The one next to the Sacristy was successively named St Thomas of Canterbury's Chapel, the Count and Countess's Chapel, the Chapel of the Relics and the Chapel of Ecce Homo (this reputedly miraculous image was disposed in 1624 after the reconstruction organized in 1613-19 by Archbishop Fernando de Acebedo). The chapel that opened onto the ambulatory and the transept was originally dedicated to St Mary Magdalen, to whose advowson St Andrew's was added in 1445.

The Chapel today, occupying two sections of the ambulatory and with access from the transept, was promoted in 1670 as his funerary chapel by Archbishop Enrique de Peralta y Cárdenas, who engaged Juan de la Sierra Bocerráiz and Bernabé de Hazas to plan the work, which was to respect the style of the recent Chapel of Ecce Homo, or Chapel of the Relics and lengthen it into the adjoining chapel. Marble, alabaster, slate and bronze are the materials which give colour to the piece, one of great dignity within the Classicism of the 17th Century, the whole being covered by two domes, the first one being heightened with a lantern.

The funerary *arcosolium* is disposed on the right, perhaps a courtesan project, its Classicist architecture including the prelate's shield and his praying effigy in bronze kneeling before his prie-dieu, an extraordinary piece of Hispanic funerary art of the period.

The main altarpiece of the chapel is typical of its time, its gilding and polychromy being commissioned from Alonso Alvarez Ruyales in 1671 by means of a contract in which Master Policarpo de Nestosa - perhaps the maker of the piece - appears as his guarantor. It is a one-story ensemble with wreathed columns, the main niche of which holds a valuable "Ecce Homo", attributable to Gil de Siloe, flanked in the intercolumns by angels, while an image of the Emperor St Henry, patron saint of the Archbishop, occupies the semicircular top finished off with the episcopal shield.

The works commissioned by Archbishop Peralta include the two screens opening onto the ambulatory, made in 1671 by Antonio Salcedo, who followed the model of the early 17th Century screen giving onto the transept. The archbishop also funded the organ.

There is an altarpiece with fluted columns, typical of the third quarter of the 17th Century, which contains late Gothic statues of St Andrew and Mary Magdalen.

There is also evidence of earlier burials and other funeral activity here. Such is the case of some 13th Century altarfronts disposed on the wall and thought to have belonged to Bishops of Burgos. There are two sepulchres with *arcosolia*. One of them, a Gothic one, is that of Canon Juan García de Medina de Pomar (d. 1492), a member of the circle of the High Constable and his wife, who is represented reclining under a baskethandle arch over which curved tracery with *crockets* serves as a pedestal for the Calvary group. The piece may be the work of Simon of Cologne's workshop. Next to it we can see the sepulchre of Canon Abaunza (d. 1554), a Renaissance piece with a relief of the Wailing for the Dead Christ behind the canon's reclining effigy. Above this there is a niche with the Annunciation, presided over by God the Father in the pediment, the whole topped out by the Calvary scene, while St John the Baptist and St Andrew are present at the sides.

Top: *"Ecce Homo" Emotive image from the end of the 15th Century, attributable to Gil de Siloe.*

Bottom: *Dome of St Henry's Chapel. Noble materials and Classicist lines lend great dignity to this 17th Century work.*

The Southern Arm of the Transept

The lie of the land on which the Cathedral is built, and the morphology of the building have determined that only one chapel be built on each side of the southern arm of the transept: St Henry's, also reached from the ambulatory, and the Chapel of the Visitation.

THE ENTRANCE TO THE CLOISTERS

It is interesting to admire, however, in the west wall, the portal (normally closed) giving access to the cloisters, an extraordinary monumental piece from the end of the 13th Century, perhaps worked on by Master Juan Pérez (d. 1296). It has been linked with Franco-Champagne sculpture. The tympanum shows the Baptism of Christ, together with two groups of people, perhaps in reference to the call of the disciples. The temporal genealogy of Christ, the tree of Jesse and the prophets are to be seen in the 14 figures arranged on two archivolts, the outer

Door to the Cloister, from the Transept.

In the southern arm of the transept, stands this remarkable Gothic door, built around 1260-80. Its architectural structure is echoed many times in the region, as are the heraldic motifs on it. It is dedicated to the Coming of Christ as a man. The prophet Isaiah and King David, on the right-hand jamb, foretell His arrival, announced by the angel to Mary on the left-hand jamb. Mary's genealogy of kings and prophets is shown on the archivolts, while the tympanum is given over to the Baptism of Jesus. Apart from its expressive beauty, it is interesting to note the ideological relationship with the Monarchy of Castile-León with religion, brought out by Christ's royal lineage.

Leaves of the door to the cloister. Around 1492-95, these doors were made, perhaps the work of Gil de Siloe, where several saints and the arms of Bishop Luis de Acuña accompany scenes of Christ's Entry into Jerusalem and his Descent into Limbo.

one, decorated with vegetables, resting on two corbels, each with a head (local tradition identifies one of them as St Francis, who would have passed through Burgos founding monasteries). On the jambs there are beautiful sculptures concerning Christ's coming; on the left there is a group of the Annunciation with a smiling angel, artistically linked with the west face of Reims Cathedral, while on the left we can see two prophets, Isaiah and David, announcing the coming of Jesus. On the other hand, a notable curiosity is the medieval association of Christ with the monarchy, which is made patent in the shields of castles and lions which, following the Mudejar taste for repetitions, are to be seen around the jambs and lintel.

The double wooden door itself is later, being made towards the end of the 15th Century, as is indicated by the style of its carving and the presence on each part of the arms of Bishop Luis Acuña (1457-95). They seem to be the work of Gil de Siloe, who worked for that prelate, and were carved in the period 1492-95. Each leaf of the door has two tiers of Gothic tracery, the lower one dedicated to St Peter and St Paul, and the upper one to scenes of Christ's Entry in Jerusalem and his Descent into Limbo.

THE CHAPEL OF THE VISITATION

Opposite this door is the Chapel of the Visitation, founded for his burial and that of his ecclesiastical relatives by Bishop Alonso de Cartagena (1435-56). An educated man from a Jewish family, he had the anecdotal distinction of succeeding his own father, Bishop Pablo de Santamaría, who, as Rabbi of the city, had had several children before being converted to Christianity. His son Alonso de Cartagena was not only a prolific writer of Castilian proto-humanism, but was also responsible for the last stage of Gothic development of Burgos Cathedral. Apart from other works, he commissioned the architect John of Cologne to build his funerary chapel on the land then occupied by St Marina's Chapel, which was done over the period 1440-42. Later on, in 1521, the little sacristy was added by Masters Nicolás de Vergara the Elder and Juan de Matienzo.

It is important to notice that the sepulchre is uncovered, in the centre of the chapel, as it is one of the earliest examples of this arrangement, which would later be copied by eminent people. It appears to be from the studio of John of Cologne, or the "lapicidal" Pedro Fernández de Ampuero, mentioned as the executor of other works commissioned by the prelate in his will of 1453, in which the bishop expresses his desire to rest "in monumento illo quod sepultura mea fabricata est" (he died in 1456). The sepulchre cannot originally have had a reclining effigy, however, as an inventory drawn up in 1488 states that there was a large jet cross on it that the deceased had acquired in León. The recumbent form, somewhat larger than the base, was to be made some time later, around 1490-95 and, judging from the thorough, precious, style, noticeable in the skill and suggestion of qualities to be observed in the crozier, the mitre or the chasuble, by Gil de Siloe.

The base of the sepulchre is of stone, but alabaster was chosen for the effigy. The base is high, with the ends and sides adorned with reliefs separated by Gothic tracery. At the head is the Visitation, and at the feet, the Imposition of the chasuble on St Ildefonso, Marianist subjects favoured by the prelate's family and by the prelate himself, who had his patron saint included in the second of them. Next to them is the family shield, with the fleur de lys. On the right, St Peter and St Paul appear flanked by the Fathers of the Church St Ambrose and St Augustine on one side, and y St Jerome and St Gregory on the other. The left-hand side shows locally revered saints: St Lesmes, St Vítores, St John de Ortega, St Dominic de Guzmán, St Casilda and St Ursula. Several shields with the family's fleur de lys are interspersed on the plinth and on the ends. An inscription along the edge of the base says: "DILECTVS DEO ET HOMINIBVS CIVIS MEMORIA IM BENEDICTIONE EST". On the base there lies the alabaster effigy of Don Alonso. He is attired ceremoniously, with minute attention to detail, especially in the Gothic tracery of the crozier, where the bishop himself is carved praying before the Virgin, and the suggestion of embroideries on the mitre representing the Annunciation, with more on the chasuble depicting St Peter, St Paul and the scene of the Visitation. At his feet, an acolyte holds an open book, with the naturalist detail of fingers between the pages.

On a pillar in the chapel there is an angel with two shields at his feet, one with the fleur de lys and one with the letters SM, standing for the surname Santa María and for the bishop's Marianist devotion. The angel is holding an open scroll with a long Latin inscription relating some of the artistic, literary, diplomatic and religious merits (including his pilgrimage to Santiago) of the prelate, who died in his fortified residence at Villasandino in 1456, at the age of 71.

In this same chapel there are other sepulchres, on which the heraldic presence of the fleur de lys guarantees kinship with Don Alonso de Cartagena. In the rear part, on the right of the entrance, is that of his nephew Alfonso Rodríguez de Maluenda (d. 1453), on the front of which is the Calvary scene, flanked by two

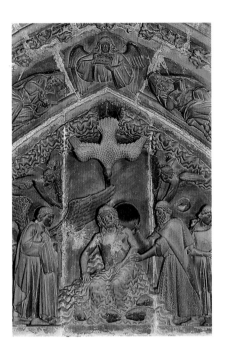

Details of the portal of the cloister: the Baptism of Jesus (on the tympanum) and the genealogy of kings and prophets (on the archivolts).

83

family shields; and at the back of the *arcosolium*, which is divided into three panels, are St Peter and St Paul, accompanied by the Fathers of the Church St Ambrose and St Jerome, together with St Gregory and St Augustine; the sides of the *arcosolium* bear St John the Baptist at the head, and, at the feet, the then recently canonized St Bernardino of Sienna, with mitres on the floor and the sign of the name of Jesus. Next to it is the tomb of García Ruiz de la Mota (d. 1507), with a remarkable tympanum showing the Virgin of the Misericord protecting several monks and kings beneath her mantel, together with praying figures whose phylacteries say "Dominus sicut vis et scis miserere mei". An exception to the rule of only burying ecclesiastical personages is constituted by the tomb of the Bishop's namesake, the gentleman Alonso de Cartagena, who lies in military armour, his sword in his hands, on a base with the front decorated with a Calvary scene and two family shields.

Other tombs belong to the Bishop of Calahorra Juan Díaz de Coca (d. 1477), cousin of the chapel's founder, and the Burgos canon and Chaplain of the Visitation Luis Garcés de Maluenda, his lying effigy sculpted in slate, as was very typical of Burgos.

The chapel preserves a simple neo-Classical altarpiece of 1780, which serves as a frame for the picture of the "Imposition of the Chasuble on St Ildefonso" painted by Manuel Martínez Barranco. There is also, hanging on the wall, a great canvass of the "The Conquest of Granada" painted at the end of the 19th Century by the painter of historical subjects Carlos Luis de Ribera (the signature is "C. L. RIBERA 1890").

Tomb of Bishop Alonso de Cartagena (d. 1456)

It lies in the centre of the Chapel of the Visitation, which he founded. The base is thought to have been made in his lifetime, and another master - perhaps Gil de Siloe - later sculpted the reclining form. The quality is remarkable, as is the precision of the details. On the front of the base there are several figures, including St Augustine, St Peter, St Paul and St Jerome. At the bottom we can also see the fleur de lys, in the family shield.

Apart from Don Gonzalo's tomb, in the Chapel of the Visitation, other interments were arranged. The most striking of them is against the abutment, that of the protonotary Canon Diego Bilbao (d. 1540), whose reclining effigy is seen before a pious group mourning for Christ.

The Southern Aisle of the Nave

Given the proximity of the old Romanesque cloisters and the Archbishop's palace, some of the old chapels of the aisle of the Epistle were renewed with the passage of time.

THE CHAPEL OF ST JOHN OF SAHAGUN

The nearest chapel to the transept is that of St John of Sahagún, which still preserves its Gothic architecture, with nerved vaults adorned with numerous shields of the Rojas family, who had been buried here since the 14th Century. In the middle ages it was called St Catherine's Chapel, or the Rojas' Chapel, but since 1765 it has had the advowson of St John of Sahagún, a 15th Century Burgos canon who later became an Augustinian friar and died in Salamanca in 1478. He was canonized in the 17th Century, when his old cathedral of Burgos took part in the ceremonies, and a relic was brought here, devotion to this saint being approved in 1647. In the 18th Century, when the neighbouring St Peter's Chapel, where his services had been taking place, became the Tabernacle of the Relics, his devotion was moved to the Rojas' Chapel, which has therefore been the Chapel of St John of Sahagún since 1765.

The altarpiece, planned by José Cortés, was made in the years 1766-70 by the architect Fernando González de Lara and the gilder Andrés Carazo, with his son, Juan Carazo. The piece is endowed with a certain animation at the base, thanks to the use of curves, several patterns of chippings on the Gothic columns and other parts. The niche contains an extraordinary image of the Saint by the sculptor Juan Pascual de Mena. At the top there is a rather heavy-looking relief dedicated to St Peter's Vision at Joppa by the Burgos carver Manuel Romero the Elder.

THE CHAPEL OF THE RELICS

From the old chapel of the Rojas, we enter the adjoining Chapel of the Relics, dedicated before the 18th Century to St Peter. The new chapel is of Baroque construction with Rococo decoration. It was planned by Friar José de San Juan de la Cruz and built in 1761-63 by Fernando González de Lara, who was also paid for the plasterwork on the ceiling, where we can see St John of Sahagún, St Telmo, St Julian, St Indalecio, Virtues and Allegories. The same González de Lara made the three reliquaries to contain the relics of the saints venerated in the Cathedral and other objects, among which a ring is mentioned which is said to have belonged to the Virgin. The most important of the works of art in the chapel is the 13th Century Gothic image of the "Virgin of Oca", painted holding the Child in her arms with a fruit and a bird in His hands.

Against the wall of this southern aisle is the *arcosolium* of the tomb of Archbishop Manuel de Castro Alonso (d. 1944) containing the praying effigy of this modern Burgos prelate. The tastes of the period resort to a Classical model, executed by Valeriano Martínez, the sculpture being done by his son Andrés Martínez Abelenda, as is indicated by the little inscription: "ANDRES MARTI-NEZ/BURGOS/MCMLII".

CHAPEL OF THE PRESENTATION

It is the most notable funerary chapel built in the early 16th Century, in the wake of the High Constable's Chapel, which it seeks to emulate - understandably so, given the arrogant personality of Canon Gonzalo de Lerma, who was the Chapter's representative at the Pontifical Court, and whose brother was Burgos

Vault of the Chapel of the Presentation.

The taste for sumptuous chapels built after the High Constable's is echoed in this one erected in 1519-24 by Juan de Matienzo for Canon Gonzalo de Lerma. Spacious and bright, it is covered with a stellate vault with tracery at the centre, over a tier of windows.

city treasurer. This chapel, dedicated to the Consolation and Presentation, was built in 1519-24 by Master Juan de Matienzo over a large square groundplan. There is a stellate vault with openwork at the apex built over an octagon supported by four squinches with scallopings at their bases containing reliefs of the evangelists. The chapel is connected to the adjoining Chapel of Christ by two arches, for which screens were commissioned from Master Pedro in 1524, but access is from the aisle through two wide arches protected by screens ordered from Cristóbal de Andino in 1528.

In the centre of the chapel lies the alabaster tomb of Don Gonzalo de Lerma, commissioned from the sculptor Philippe de Bigarny in 1524 on the condition it would be finished the following year. It echoes in some way Diego de Siloe's example for Bishop Acuña in this cathedral, but one notable difference is a high base, though still with claws at the bases of the corners, while the sides slope outwards to the bottom and are adorned with medallions showing Virtues, St Francis and St Jerome. The canon lies on top, dressed according to his status and sculpted as in death, his eyes closed and his hands in an attitude of prayer. The ensemble is effected with the technical virtuosity and softness characteristic of the Burgundian's work, the wrinkled face being especially remarkable as the canon may have sat for it, for he did not die until January 1527.

There are other Renaissance tombs in the chapel. Against the inside abutment is that of the protonotary Canon Gonzalo Bilbao (d. 1540), who had it constructed here while still alive because of his friendship with the founder and because he was head chaplain of the chapel. Behind his effigy reclining on its base there is a sort of altarpiece with Plateresque designs. Its first tier shows the group of Mourners for Christ, flanked by St Dominic de la Calzada and St John the Baptist, while the second one has a Virgin and Child with medallions of St Peter and St Paul, the whole crowned with a bust of God the Father. Opposite the altar-

Following two pages: *Sepulchre of Canon Gonzalo de Lerma.*

The canon's tomb, commissioned from Philippe de Bigarny in 1524, is as eminent as those of bishops. Don Gonzalo's stormy personality is reflected in the face of his effigy. The high plinth is decorated with saints and virtues: St Jerome strikes his chest before the skull; Prudence has two faces: the rear one that of a bearded man with experience of the past, and the front one that of a girl looking to the future and seeing herself in a mirror; Hope looks up with her hands together in prayer.

87

piece and to its left there is an *arcosolium* over the tomb of Don Juan Lerma (d. 1546) and his wife. To the right of the altarpiece we can see two *arcosolia* with foundations of Canon Alonso Díez de Lerma, the founder's nephew, who had another *arcosolium* built on the right after 1553, dedicated to the Apostles St Simon and St Jude, to the Eleven Thousand Virgins and to St Elizabeth of Hungary.

The altarpiece is of simple neo-Classical architecture and contains two remarkable works. The great painting of the Holy Family is an example of the Renaissance work of the Venetian Sebastiano del Piombo, perhaps brought from Italy by Don Gonzalo de Lerma himself, for the year after his death, in a Visit to the Chapel in 1528, mention is made of "a great image of Our Lady being used as an altarpiece", possibly in reference to this picture. The sculpture of St Joseph with the Child, paid for in 1782, is attributed to Juan Pascual de Mena, perhaps from his latest period, judging form the neo-Classical air of the piece.

Among other works, there is a painting of St John the Baptist, considered to be a Bolognese work of the second quarter of the 17th Century.

THE CHAPEL OF THE CHRIST OF BURGOS

The last chapel of the southern aisle of the nave is that of the Christ of Burgos. This advowson is a recent one, instigated in the wake of the 19th Century Disentailment of Church property, as a result of which, in 1835, the

The Chapel of the Holy Christ of Burgos.

In the 19th Century, because of the Disentailment of Church property, in 1835 this devout image was installed in an elongated chapel, whose sides are lined with tombs.

Bottom: *Virgin and Child, in the Chapel of the Holy Christ.*

A beautiful Gothic sculpture of a standing Mary with her son, also upright, in her arms, establishing a loving mother-child relationship.

famous image of Christ Crucified was brought in from St Augustine's Convent, situated outside the city wall, where it had been an object of devotion. It appears to take up a large part of what was a corridor of the old cloister, where we know that as early as 1285, there was a chapel with the advowson of the Holy Cross. At the beginning of the 17th Century it was known as the Chapel of Our Lady of the Remedies, as her effigy was inside the door, while during that century, images were added of Christ Crucified and Christ tied to the Column, so in 1633 it became the Chapel of the Holy Christ of the Remedies. In time it acquired a cross-shaped groundplan, with a very long nave and two side chapels off its penultimate section. Indeed, the one on the left was commissioned by the executors of the will of Dean Luis de Quintanadueñas from Master Juan de Ribas in 1644. In the 19th Century, as has been said, the Christ of Burgos was brought here from St Augustine's Monastery, and alterations were carried out at the end of the century by the architect Vicente Lampérez.

The neo-Gothic altarpiece contains an image of the Holy Christ, of the in-pain type common in the 14th Century, this example being of wood covered with leather, with wounds and with beard, hair and nails attached.

On a shelf in the presbytery, on the right-hand side, there is a beautiful standing image in polychromed stone of the Virgin and Child, apparently an early 14th Century Gothic piece. Another Gothic image, also in stone, is of the Virgin of the Remedies, a 13th Century seated Mother and Child disposed over the inside of the door.

The side walls of the chapel nave bear memorial stones and tombs of prelates and chapter prebendaries, mainly of the 14th and 19th Centuries, as was determined by the architect Lampérez at the end of the 19th Century. Over the tomb of Don Pedro Berrantes de Aldana, who died in 1658, there was placed an allegory of Charity by the sculptor José Alcoverro, as a symbol of the merits of the promoter of the hospital named after him.

The Cloister and Museum

Today the Cloister is normally entered from the Museum via the anteroom to the sacristy, although there is a 13th Century monumental door, mentioned in the section about the southern arm of the transept.

The Building of the Cloister has been dated in the 13th Century and beginning of the 14th. An original feature is its division into two stories, a result of the conditions imposed by the lie of the land. The architecture can be appreciated from the outside if the observer uses the lower pathway, which relieves the pedestrian traffic of Paloma Street.

There are only chapels on the west side of the cloister: those of St John the Baptist, or of the Treasury, St Catherine and Corpus Christi, plus the Chapter House, for the northern corridor shares a wall with the sacristy and the chapels off the ambulatory, while of the other two sides one borders the transept and the other is the outer boundary wall.

When Don Manuel de Castro Alonso was prelate (1928-44), a Cathedral Museum was established, displaying important works of the church together with other pieces from the diocese, on the upper floor of the cloister and its chapels.

The cloister contains several monumental sculptures which were made for it. Among them are the groups disposed on the corner piers, where we find the Annunciation with two Prophets, the Adoration of the Magi, and two other groups, one of which is interpreted as Ferdinand III and Don Mauricio with collaborators, and the other as four princes, sons of Alfonso X. On the walls of the cloister there are several large statues of saints and bishops, including the original of the mullion of the *Sarmental* Door and two others thought to be Alfonso X and his wife Doña Violante.

Off the cloister is the Chapel of St John the Baptist, which had been build by Bishop Juan Cabeza de Vaca (1406-12) for his burial, but the present structure dates from the 16th Century, when alterations were made, at the same time as those to the adjoining St James's Chapel, as has been mentioned, so the existing chapel is the work of Juan de Vallejo. At the time, Renaissance recesses were incorporated into the walls to house the original reclining sculptures. Today, it is a Museum, where there are many extraordinary pieces on show, especially cloths and silverwork.

There are two more chapels with remarkable doors which follow the example of the cloister entrance door, even in their heraldic motifs. St Catherine's Chapel, begun in 1326 by Bishop Gonzalo de Hinojosa, the tympanum over whose door shows Christ Taken Down from the Cross, attended by a group of people mourning, is characteristic of the expressiveness of the first half of the 14th Century. Over the inside there is an attractive stellate vault resting on corbels with polychrome reliefs. The great size of this vault reflects that of the earlier Chapter

House at Oña and is in turn reflected by the later Barbazana Chapel at Pamplona. St Catherine's Chapel was used as a chapter house, and was also occasionally used for meetings of the city council until a noble sacristy was formed here by Archbishop Navarrete at the beginning of the 17th Century. In it a portrait gallery of Burgos prelates was created, where there are works by such painters as Diego de Leiva, Mateo Cerezo, Nicolás de la Cuadra, and Friar Gregorio de Barambio. There is also a rich Baroque chest of drawers by Friar Pedro Martínez, a Benedictine from Cardeña, commissioned by Archbishop Samaniego. Other works of art in this chapel include statues and goldwork.

Next door is the Chapel of Corpus Christi, founded by the soldier and diplomat Juan Estébanez. The tympanum over the door repeats a subject frequently used in Gothic Burgos, the Deesis, here accompanied by two additional praying figures - Estébanez and his wife - sculpted on the lintel together with their armorial bearings.

Inside the chapel we can see the tomb of a gentleman, in the centre of the floor, with a reclining alabaster image with no inscription, which leads us to believe that it is neither García Fernández de Castellanos, the chapel founder's son, or the founder himself. Furthermore, in this chapel there are two *arcosolia* under the stairway leading up to the Records Department. Under one of them, which has a pointed arch, there is the tomb of Miguel Esteban de Huerto del Rey and his wife Doña Ucenda, whose reclining effigies are of the late 13th Century, the man being represented with a large two-handed sword in his hands, and the woman with a rosary. Under the second *arcosolium*, two tombs dating from the second third of the 16th Century have been put together: those of Aldonza de la Vega, lady of Aguilar, and Garci Fernández Manrique, the first Count of Castañeda, two people who had founded outside St Giles' wall the Monastery of the Trinity, where they were buried. The tombs follow the model used for the High Constable and may be attributed to Juan de Lugano, or Master Angelo Bagut and Master Bartolomé Carlone.

What is most noteworthy is the polychrome wooden statue of Christ tied to the column, a work by Diego de Siloe in which the Renaissance sculptor shows

Sculpture groups in the cloister.

There are several groups on the corner piers of the cloister. One is interpreted as the founders of the Gothic building, Bishop Mauricio and King Ferdinand III, with two princes. Another is the Adoration of the Magi, one of whom is kneeling before Jesus, held in His mother's arms, while St Joseph remains withdrawn from the scene, as was normal in medieval ideology.

his expressive ability by endowing the naked body with a feeling of pain. According to popular tradition, the chest disposed at the top of the wall is El Cid's famous Coffer, mentioned in heroic literature. There are several other tombs and funerary memorials in the cloister of Gothic or Renaissance taste. A Gothic tympanum with the "Deesis" must have belonged to one of them. The oldest interment, with a multifoiled arch, is from the late 12th Century and comes from the Monastery of St Peter of Arlanza (according to one tradition it is that of the avenging Mudarra). The late Gothic tomb of Canon Gonzalo de Burgos (d. 1509) is especially interesting, with the original subject of Jesus with the Samaritan on its front and the Resurrection of Christ in the *arcosolium*. But perhaps greater artistic fame is enjoyed by the Renaissance tomb of Canon Santander (d. 1523) by the sculptor Diego de Siloe, with an elegant composition of the Virgin and Child behind the lying effigy of the prebendary resting on a simple urn.

Among the pieces kept in the Museum, several are worthy of especial note. One very old piece is the altar front and reredos from Mave (until recently part of the Diocese of Burgos, now under the See of Palencia) which can be dated in the second quarter of the 13th Century, with the Pantocrator and Tetramorph accompanied by the Apostles. There are also several Gothic images of the Virgin and Child and other later sculptures.

Some silver-gilt images with relics of St Peter, St Paul and St James, commissioned from Juan González Frías, were made for Bishop Luis de Acuña (1456-95), as his shield indicates.

A stone relief of "Christ in Majesty" must be from a keystone, and the one of "Jesus Healing the Blind Man" is obviously from a tympanum.

Left: *Door of Corpus Christi Chapel, in the cloister. An echo of the* Coronería *Door is to be seen in the "Deesis" on the tympanum, the architectural scheme of the main Cloister Door being repeated here.*

Top and bottom: *Canons' tombs in the cloister: the Renaissance one of Gaspar de Illescas and the late Gothic one of Gonzalo de Burgos.*

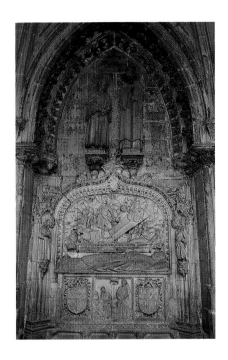

There are examples of medieval Flemish paintings here: the "Virgin and Child from the 'Beautiful Country'" by a Brussels artists of the circle of Van der Weyden mentioned in the historiography as the "Master of the Embroidered Foliage" and the "Virgin and Child", representing the art of Hans Memling.

The remains of the Altarpiece of the old Chapel of the Relics are quite remarkable, with scenes of Christ's life and passion, made at the end of the 15th Century to keep all the relics which the Cathedral had amassed in the Middle Ages. While the relics had been previously kept in the sacristy, the new altarpiece-cum-reliquary was placed in the adjoining chapel, where the Counts of Carrión were buried, which was to be named New Chapel of the Relics or the Chapel of St Thomas of Canterbury. In the 17th Century, the reliquary was moved into the sacristy. It comprised in fact a sort of large cupboard, which could be closed, adorned with paintings, some of them on the sides and others on the doors, which were painted inside and out. An old testimony says that it was "an altarpiece with doors, which for greater decency were kept closed". This retable was taken down after being replaced by three new ones in 1763. Several of its boards were kept in the Cathedral, and have been in the Museum since 1930.

The paintings were commissioned by Chapter members from Alonso de Sedano as is recorded by the payment made to him in 1495, but discrepancies between the painter and the Chapter in 1496 led to a delay in meeting full payment, which was not made until 1500. On this retable, Alonso de Sedano had the collaboration of the so-called "Master of the Balbases". Nine scenes from the retable are preserved in the Cathedral, seven of which are attributed to Alonso de Sedano and two to the "Master of the Balbases". This master painted one side of a

95

Door of St Catherine's Chapel, in the cloister.

It follows the pattern of the cloister entrance door, with similar heraldic decoration; the tympanum shows an expressive scene of Christ Taken Down from the Cross.

Bottom: *El Cid's chest, in Corpus Christi Chapel. Tradition considers it to be one of the two "red leather chests with gilt nails" mentioned in the poem in the ruse to get money from Raquel and Vidas, Jews of Burgos.*

board with the "Nativity of Christ" (the other side bears the "Crowning with Thorns" by Alonso de Sedano). The scene, which includes in the background the Tidings brought to the Shepherds, shows the Child on the ground in the foreground, being worshipped by an angel, and His mother, with a choir of angels intoning songs and St Joseph approaching with a candle whose flame he is shielding with his hand. If the Child is visually outstanding because His pale naked body is laid on the dark mantle of the Virgin, she is brought out by the brocade held behind her by angels. The scene is set before the ruins of a Roman arch, under which we can see the manger with the ass and the ox, in obvious reference to the Old Testament passage where Isaiah prophesies that "The ox knows its owner and the ass its master's stall". Another composition by the Master of the Balbases is the "Arrest of Christ", inspired in part by engravings by Ian van Zwolle and, especially, by Schongauer. A mob surrounds Jesus, hitting Him and pushing Him in order to take Him away, but He remains patient, and is worried about Malcus, who is lying on the floor and whom Jesus approaches to replace the ear cut off by St Peter with a sword which he now sheathes.

Seven scenes are by Alonso de Sedano. A board painted on both sides represents the Annunciation and the Lashes. In the "Annunciation" he adds to Gabriel a retinue of angels, a rare detail, as is also the fact that the dove is preceded by a winged Christchild, constituting a Trinity, with God the Father visible in the sky through the upper window. The painting of the "Lashes", linked with an engraving by Schongauer, shows Jesus tied to the column and whipped by torturers before Pilate and his retinue.

View of a pathway in the cloister, with sculptures and tombs.

Following page: *Marian imagery in the Cathedral.*

There are many Marian sculptures from different parts of the diocese, At the top is Our Lady of Oca, an interesting evocation of the early medieval forerunners of the Diocese of Burgos, although the sculpture is a very correct Gothic piece reminiscent of 13th Century models. The lower example is from the last third of the century.

Another board painted by Alonso de Sedano has on one side the "Adoration of the Magi" similar to the same subject painted by Diego de la Cruz and hanging in the Cathedral. The other side shows the "Nailing", with one torturer pulling on a rope to stretch Jesus's arm in order to nail it on, while another two are unloading their hammers before groups of onlookers; in the background is the complementary scene of Christ's tunic being played for with dice, while in the distance the process culminates in Calvary.

The "Crowning with Thorns" is also by Alonso de Sedano (on the other side is the Nativity by the Master of the Balbases), the subject being common in the 15th Century because of the devotion to the Holy Thorn, which many Christian shrines sought to have. The crowning takes place inside Pilate's palace, with Jesus seated and several minions wounding and mocking Him, as in one of Schongauer's engravings. His physical pain is aggravated by the moral pain of the betrayal by St Peter, who in a marginal scene on the left is denying Christ, a forced inclusion of an episode which was earlier in time.

In the "Ecce Homo", Jesus, whipped, crowned and covered with a purple robe, is at the gates of the Praetorium, behind which is Pilate, who hands Him over to the soldiers and the priests, who revile Him and demand His crucifixion, as in Schongauer's engraving; a curious note is the Renaissance frieze Sedano paints on the wall of the Praetorium. Another composition on this retable is the "Road to Calvary", set at the city gates of Jerusalem, which are also decorated with Renaissance motifs: in some details it also follows an engraving by Schongauer, as Veronica has relieved Christ's bloodied face with her handkerchief, on which His likeness is impressed, to which the torturers react by violently recommencing the journey.

Another remarkable work is the Triptych of the Adoration of the Magi. It was perhaps executed in 1495 by Diego de la Cruz and commissioned by the Brotherhood of God the Father, of the nearby Church of St Gadea, to which the Chapter gave permission to commemorate "in the arch where God the Father is, which is over the sepulchre of Juan Martínez Gadea, the festival of the Epiphany in perpetuum, which is in the new cloister, and for which it must be boldly painted". The middle board shows the Adoration of the Magi, while the side ones bear the Annunciation and an equestrian St Julian. The brotherhood had a hospital in its care, whence the reference to St Julian and the Magi, patrons of hospitals.

We must also remember the two paintings St Antón and the Bishop Saint, in watercolour on wood, in the Chapel of Juan Estébanez. They are the remains of a predella and are thought to have come from the school of Juan Sánchez around 1460.

Although its condition is deficient, an interesting piece is the board of St John de Ortega and the Donating Lady by the "Master of the Visitation of Palencia", which comes from the shrine of that Burgos saint and protector of the Road to Santiago.

From a reredos depicting the life of Christ, of the school of Friar Alonso de Zamora (the old master of Oña), there are two panels with paintings on each side, that is four paintings. On one side they show the angel and the Virgin in the scene of the Annunciation, and on the other, the Nativity and the Adoration of the Magi.

The pictures painted by León Picardo in 1524 for the High Constable and his wife concerning Calvary and St Vincent are Renaissance.

The best silversmiths also worked for Burgos Cathedral, though only part of their work remains, a few objects being on show in the chapels of the cloister museum, from Gothic to modern.

There is also a wealth of cloth items. Those dedicated to liturgy, such as the vestments and other altarcloths, were commissioned by the chapter or by the bishops (some examples are preserved of those donated in the 15th Century by the prelates Alonso de Cartagena and Luis de Acuña). There is also a rich group of French and Flemish tapestries, including an outstanding one depicting "Original Sin", hanging in St John's Chapel. It is a Gothic piece made in the mid 14th Century and is woven in wool and silk. Its origin is recorded in the initials BB (Brabante, Brussels).

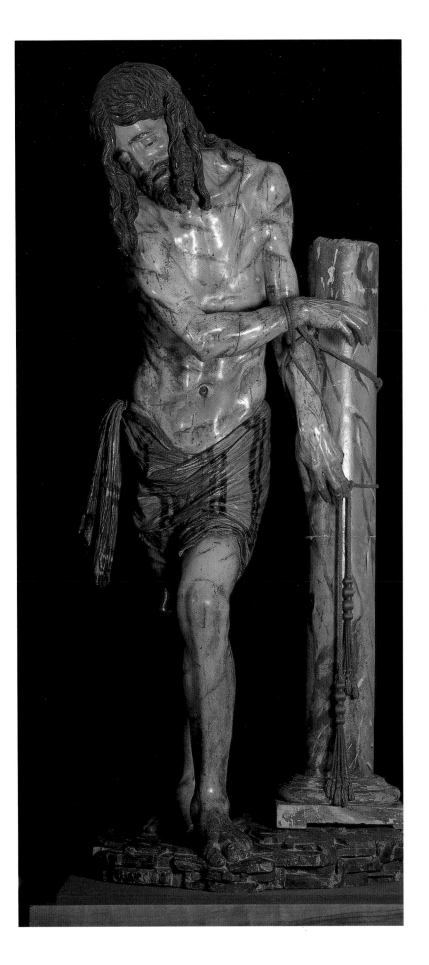

Jesus tied to the column.

This is one of the most interesting sculptures in Corpus Christi Chapel, from the gouge of Diego de Siloe, whose expressive quality it shows.

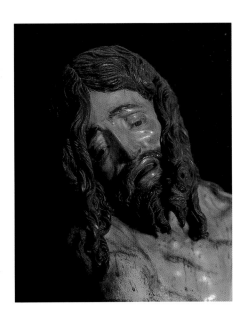

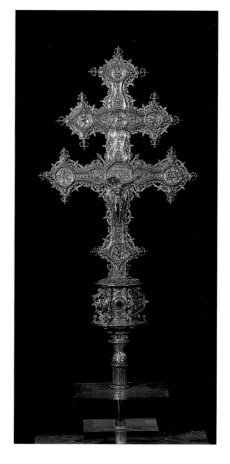

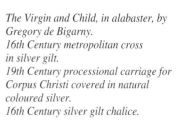

*The Virgin and Child, in alabaster, by
Gregory de Bigarny.
16th Century metropolitan cross
in silver gilt.
19th Century processional carriage for
Corpus Christi covered in natural
coloured silver.
16th Century silver gilt chalice.*

"Virgin and Child", late 15th Century, from the school of Hans Mamling. (From Ameyugo).

Neo-Gothic tabernacle, made in 1927 by the famous goldsmith Granda.

Boards belonging to the old Altarpiece of the Relics, c. 1495. The Lashes, by Alonso de Sedano. The Birth of Christ, by the Master of the Balbases.

BIBLIOGRAPHY

ANDRES ORDAX, Salvador: *Burgos*. En *Castilla y León/1*. Vol. 9 de "La España Gótica". Ed. Encuentro. Madrid, 1989.

ANDRES ORDAX, Salvador: *Arte gótico*. "Historia de Burgos". T. II, Edad Media-2. Burgos, 1987.

ANDRES ORDAX, Salvador: *Guía de Burgos*. León, 1990.

ANDRES ORDAX, Salvador: *La Provincia de Burgos*. León, 1991.

ANDRES ORDAX, Salvador: *La Catedral de Burgos*. En "Las Catedrales de Castilla y León". Edilesa. León, 1992.

AZCARATE LUXAN, Matilde: *Iconografía de los tímpanos góticos españoles*. Madrid, 1985.

AZCARATE RISTORI, José María: *Arte Gótico en España*. Madrid, 1990.

ELORZA GUINEA, Juan Carlos y BARTOLOME ARRAIZA, Alberto: *Arte medieval burgalés y esmaltes del taller de Silos y contemporáneos*. Bilbao, 1978.

GOMEZ BARCENA, María Jesús: *Escultura gótica funeraria en Burgos*. Burgos, 1988.

HUIDOBRO Y SERNA, Luciano: *La catedral de Burgos*, Madrid, 1958.

IBAÑEZ PEREZ, Alberto Cayetano: *Burgos, su pintura en el s. XV*. Bilbao, 1985.

KARGE, Henrik: *Die Kathedrale von Burgos und die Spanische Architektur des 13. Jahrhunderts. Französische Hochgotik in Kastilien und León*. Berlín, 1989.

LAMBERT, Elíe: *El arte gótico en España*. Ed. Cátedra. Madrid, 1977.

LOPEZ MATA, Teófilo: *La catedral de Burgos*. Burgos, 1962.

MARTIN GONZALEZ, Juan José (Coord.): *Las Edades del Hombre. El Arte en la Iglesia de Castilla y León*. Salamanca, 1988.

MARTIN GONZALEZ, Juan José: *Escultura barroca castellana. Segunda Parte*. Madrid, 1971.

MARTINEZ Y SANZ, M.: *Historia del Templo de la Catedral de Burgos*. Burgos, 1866 (reimp. Burgos, 1983).

REDONDO CANTERA, María José: *El sepulcro en España en el s. XVI. Tipología e Iconografía*. Madrid, 1987.

RICO, Marcos: *La Catedral de Burgos*. Burgos, 1985.

SILVA MAROTO, María Pilar: *Pintura Hispanoflamenca Castellana: Burgos y Palencia. Obras en tabla y sarga*. Valladolid, 1990.

URREA FERNANDEZ, Jesús: *La catedral de Burgos*. León, 1982.

YARZA LUACES, Joaquín: *La Edad Media*. Historia del Arte Hispánico, t. II. Madrid, 1978.

YARZA LUACES, Joaquín: *Gil de Siloe*. Madrid, 1991.

Cope

*The Cathedral still keeps part of the extraordinary
wealth of ornaments donated to it by prelates and
chapter members. This example is in 14th Century
Nazareth cloth with an inscription in thuluth script
which translates as "Glory to Our Lord the
Sultan".*